Dance Education Tips From the Trenches

Cheryl M. Willis, EdD

HUMAN KINETICS

Library of Congress Cataloging-in-Publication Data

Willis, Cheryl M.
  Dance education tips from the trenches / Cheryl M. Willis.
    p. cm.
  ISBN 0-7360-4567-8 (pbk.)
  1. Dance--Study and teaching (Elementary)--United States. 2. Dance
for children--United States. I. Title.
  GV1799.W55 2003
  372.86′8--dc21

                                                          2003005598

ISBN: 0-7360-4567-8

Acquisitions Editor: Judy Patterson Wright, PhD; **Developmental Editor:** Melissa Feld; **Assistant Editor:** Susan C. Hagan; **Copyeditor:** Joanna Hatzopoulos Portman; **Proofreader:** Julie Marx Goodreau; **Permission Manager:** Dalene Reeder; **Graphic Designer:** Robert Reuther; **Graphic Artist:** Kathleen Boudreau-Fuoss; **Cover Designer:** Jack W. Davis; **Photographer (author photo):** Bruno Studios; **Art Manager:** Kelly Hendren; **Illustrator (cover and interior):** Dick Flood, except charts 5.2 and 5.3 by Kelly Hendren; **Printer:** United Graphics

Printed in the United States of America   10   9   8   7   6   5   4   3   2   1

Human Kinetics
Web site: www.HumanKinetics.com

United States: Human Kinetics
P.O. Box 5076, Champaign, IL 61825-5076
800-747-4457
e-mail: humank@hkusa.com

Canada: Human Kinetics
475 Devonshire Road Unit 100, Windsor, ON N8Y 2L5
800-465-7301 (in Canada only)
e-mail: orders@hkcanada.com

Europe: Human Kinetics
107 Bradford Road, Stanningley, Leeds LS28 6AT, United Kingdom
+44 (0) 113 255 5665
e-mail: hk@hkeurope.com

Australia: Human Kinetics
57A Price Avenue, Lower Mitcham, South Australia 5062
08 8277 1555
e-mail: liaw@hkaustralia.com

New Zealand: Human Kinetics
Division of Sports Distributors NZ Ltd.
P.O. Box 300 226 Albany, North Shore City, Auckland
0064 9 448 1207
e-mail: blairc@hknewz.com

To my creative dance students,
who have experienced dance
as a means of joy and self-expression

Contents

PART

II

The Creative Process   129

Preface

Dance Education Tips From the Trenches is about my personal experiences in developing a creative dance program and teaching creative dance in the public school setting. My intention is to share practical organizational methods with dance educators who have had little or no experience in teaching dance to children in the public schools. I hope you will be able to reflect on my experiences as you build your own dance program.

As dance educators, we bring to the field a variety of experiences as professional dancers, choreographers, college professors, and teachers in the private sector. Our sensibilities have been highly developed and we are passionate about expressing ourselves through them. The love of dance, the desire to create, the hope of sharing dance with the next generation, and the need to acquire a livelihood propel many of us to a career in dance education.

Most of us have had dynamic courses in teaching creative dance. We have explored every aspect of space, time, and energy, and we have learned many dance games and activities through which to teach these concepts. We have developed lesson plans about dance within cultures; dance and the sciences; dance in relation to literature; dance as it evolved throughout history; dance as an expression of art; and dance to explore philosophy, religion, and psychology. However, the everyday minutiae, which are essential for survival in the public schools, are rarely addressed. If you were one of the fortunate people who were totally prepared for the challenges of public school teaching, send flowers to your professor today!

During their first year of teaching, many dance specialists are discouraged by the perplexities of the system. Many schools have overloaded classes, which could vary from 20 to 35 students in a primary class. A full-time position may require teaching 30 or more different classes a week. Time allotted for class periods may not be adjusted to the students' performance level. For example, 30 minutes may be adequate for first graders, whereas an hour may be more beneficial to fifth graders. Faculty members may consider the time their students are in dance class as a preparation period, and therefore they may not be interested in the subject matter or in assisting in class management during that time. Another task is bridging the world of the arts with a sports-oriented society, in which parents or teachers may undermine dance and its value to the children. The growing number of disturbed and drug- or alcohol-affected students presents extraordinary problems. In many instances, the dance class becomes a dumping ground for coping with inclusion; socialization; right-brained learners; physically, mentally, and emotionally challenged students; and others who are not functioning in the classroom. Moreover, dance specialists have been overwhelmed by the degree of class management required and the amount of energy demanded for the daily routine. For many dance specialists, learning to work within the public schools while preserving one's sensibilities becomes a struggle for personal survival.

The picture I paint may sound negative, but these comments have been gathered from public school creative dance teachers who, I'm happy to report, have frantically survived their first year of teaching. Most dance specialists admit that they had no idea of the personal challenges that awaited them or of the struggles necessary to develop dance programs in the public schools. Although dance specialists have been highly trained in methods of teaching creative dance, they have not yet fully explored the minutiae of teaching.

The essays in this book are not intended to be a dance curriculum or a list of dance activities, and they are not presented as an academic research study. These writings, however, are about *minutiae!* This book contains tips and information on class management and organization, logistics, methods for creating dance audiences, the creative dance process, formal and informal performances, clothing, gender differences, motivation, faculty support, the dance space, and stories—lots of stories. These narratives are about actual situations and are highlighted with the following icon: ◖◗. Many of the writings are analogies or monologues that I perform for the children. Drama is a large component of my teaching style because I find it successful with young children. I believe that a tint of humor (a required characteristic in this field!) persists throughout my writings and in my teaching style.

This book has been organized into chapters containing usable and reflective essays. The essays have been organized into the following sections for quick referral:

 Obstacles introduce a problem that you might encounter.

 Solutions provide several ideas about methods that worked or were glorious mistakes for me.

 Tips are ideas that have been proven to work.

Trench truths are stories or ideas designed to inform you about real-life experiences in dance education.

Much of the information presented in this book has been developed from my journals. Some of the ideas and methods have been shared with, stolen from, nurtured, and revised with other dance specialists. *Dance Education Tips From the Trenches* is not about the ideal, but rather about reality from my experiences and viewpoint. It contains a compilation of my experiences, opinions, and methods in dance education in the public schools.

My method of teaching has evolved through the influence of a jazz philosophy, which acknowledges a mistake not as a failure, but as an opportunity to take one to another realm. It opens one to the beauty of improvisation and to the exploration of new avenues. Although these writings express exceptionally strong opinions about teaching creative dance, my style of teaching goes with the flow—once a flow has been established. Drawing from a wide variety of teaching experiences, I am continuously exploring methods that maintain focus, class management, and the joy of dance.

Over the past 11 years, my position as a creative dance educator has evolved into a rewarding situation. I have taught in 6 elementary schools: 11 consecutive years in one school, and 1 to 4 years in other schools based on their needs. I have had the pleasure and the difficult job of introducing creative dance in 2 schools, and I also continued existing programs in the other schools. Although I teach approximately 900 students per week, there are actually many moments when I experience the "aha!" of dance, which is truly wonderful. Providing an atmosphere for these moments to flourish has evolved very, very, very slowly. By sharing my experiences and solutions, you may get there faster than I did!

Acknowledgments

I would like to acknowledge the many people who assisted in the process of writing this book: the faculty and administrators who were open to the dance experience, who were able to change any of their previous misgivings, and who were able to accept and enjoy the benefits of dance as part of the curricula; my principal of 11 years, Edna Nash, who had the ability to set the stage for a positive creative dance atmosphere and was a source of continuous support and encouragement; the dance specialists who shared their work and struggles in developing creative dance programs, especially Jän Abramovitz, Julie Brown, Betsy Claassen, Jackie Conrad, Susan Davis, Emmeley Duncan, Mary Fogarty, Amy Gaehler, Kristen Kelley, Tish Lilly, Margaret Lutz, Deb Mata, Sheyla Mattos, Bev Melum, Angela Pozzi, Rie Gilsdorf, Laura Schubothe, Rhonda Summer, Cindy Taylor, Wendy Tompson, Fern Tresvan, and Dawn Tuman; Dee Gramley and Chris Brunelle, with whom I worked as an arts team on integrated curricula, and arts team members Cindy Bluemel, Lois Ann Davisson, Carol Goodson, Nancy Heine, Rosemary Muto, Jennifer Porter, and Jan Taylor-Taskey; Deb Brzoska for her contributions to dance education at the district, state, and national levels; Anne Green Gilbert for her support and continuous encouragement; Jän Abramovitz, JoAnn Amberg, Betsy Claassen, Maria Fama, Audrey Jung, and Sally Mundinger for sharing their professional knowledge with me; my professors, Sr. Mary Estelle Foucheaux, MSC, and Dr. Sarah Hilsendager, for their patient guidance; Daniella Jay and Sharon Friedler for advising me about publishing; Carolyn Ollikainen, Molly Zinda, Kathy Warren, and Sandy Rasmussen for continuous assistance with technological skills; and to my friends who have discussed, argued about, philosophized about, read, and edited this book: Dr. Nancy Baron, Dr. Elaine Breshgold, Maria Fama, Stefani Galaday, Candance Kagan, and Susan Starkey—thanks for your time, energy and encouragement!

This work is an extension of articles written for *The Journal of Physical Education, Recreation, and Dance* (April, May/June, and August 1995). While some of the information on gender, poverty, and parent education is the same, the format, style, and extension of the material is different.

Prelude

The Dance

It was a night performance of third, fourth and fifth graders. The auditorium was filled with parents and friends who were enjoying the arts program, *Ancient Symbols of Winter*. The students danced through rays of stage light, depicting the darkness of winter.

As the third graders performed, I temporarily forgot my role as dance director and lighting designer. I became mesmerized by the all-out movement of their little bodies—a continuous flow of up and down, together and apart; contrasted with the energy of slowly expanding and quickly contracting, exploding and sustaining, resolving and ebbing again.

I was completely in the moment when a thought crept into my mind: How did they do this? It was as if I were on the outside looking in. Or could it have been that I was so completely captivated that I had forgotten the process? As I slowly pulled myself out of the trance, I realized that the dance lived and was an entity within itself. Although each student contributed to the flow, the dance was balanced by the oneness of the students' energies. It was the "aha!"—the miracle of the moment.

During the next few days I discussed the performance with the class. I tried to talk about the miracle of the moment, but I was too overwhelmed by emotion. The students seemed to be pleased with their accomplishments. They expressed that they had been scared of performing but then became so involved in the dance that they forgot their fears and enjoyed themselves. When I finally shared my feelings, they sat in wide-eyed amazement. The room was silent for several moments, and then a boy said, "It was as if you were in Wonderland." He understood my experience, and the other students did too. I wrote in my journal, "For a moment we had experienced the miracle of dance."

When analyzing the creative process that led to this performance, I questioned myself: What changed the dance on the night of the program? What was my teaching role in the process? Why was *Ancient Symbols of Winter* different from other performances? What was the creative process of dance and performance that I had taught, emphasized, and encouraged? What were the conscious and subconscious effects that dance had thus far on the lives of the students?

I reflected on the past six years I had spent with the students in this community—the many, many steps involved in their learning to perform; the long period of teaching before results were visible; and the conscious and subconscious effects that dance had had on the lives of the students and on my own life.

The ABCs of Dance Education

When I arrived in the Northwest to teach dance, the dance program was new to the curricula. My journey to the Wonderland experienced during the *Ancient Symbols of Winter* (discussed in the prelude) was an arduous path. The task of teaching the students, parents, and educators the knowledge necessary to appreciate and hopefully to accept dance was like scaling Mount Rainier.

Although I had taught dance at colleges and in the private sector, the public school environment presented many new challenges. In the private sector the students were eager to participate in dance classes. They chose to be there and the parents were happy to financially support their child's dance education. The atmosphere was relaxed and students were on a first-name basis with the teacher. There was little need to discipline the students, and the teacher had an opportunity to know each of the students personally. When the students tired of dance or became interested in other things, they quit and moved on; sometimes, they came back when they were refreshed.

In the public schools most of the students were not attending dance classes with a burning desire to be a ballet dancer or a Broadway performer, nor did they lie awake at night with a longing to experience the creative process. Dance was not a choice for them. Every student (unless excused because of religion) was either obligated or privileged to attend creative dance class. Many did not want to be there, and these students were able to make class time unbearable. Part of my role as a dance educator was that of a salesperson—trying to convince hundreds of students that dance would be the most wonderful experience of their lives.

After a few years filled with passion, determination, and persistence, the majority of students bought into the program. By the end of the fourth year, the first and second graders grew to be fourth and fifth graders with an excited attitude about dance. The transformation was beginning, but the work was unrelenting depending on the class, the school, and the administrative support.

The process of arriving in the Wonderland of the *Ancient Symbols of Winter* was not an easy one. I kept a journal that traced many of my experiences, my successes, and my mistakes. Hopefully, the information I share in part I will provide you with a map of how to get to Wonderland. The writings give you an overview of the early days of the program, and they introduce matters you will need to consider when you begin teaching dance. There are tips on managing your students; ideas on planning, organizing, and setting up for a successful class; and personal suggestions for the dance educator. And there are stories, lots of stories. Enjoy.

CHAPTER

A Rude Awakening

Why Don't They Move?

We sometimes assume that kids can't dance because they're uncoordinated. But culture, not physical ability, is one of the most significant factors influencing our ability to dance. Growing up in New Orleans, where dance was a part of the local culture, I assumed that everyone could dance. I was wrong to assume this. After living in various parts of the United States, I have been awakened to the fact that dance is not intrinsic to all Americans. Its value in this country wavers, and it has not yet evolved as a characteristic of Main Street, USA.

When I introduced creative dance to students in two elementary schools in a city in the Northwest, my expectation was for the students to hear pop music and burst into dance, the room rocking with their rhythm as they got down and boogied. I was wrong! The experience in this community was the opposite. The students looked at each other, giggled, hid behind each other, and put their heads down while their faces expressed total fear and embarrassment.

So, my first goal was to provide a safe, nurturing environment in which children could develop an appreciation and enjoyment of movement. But a series of initial student concerns that hid behind behavioral smoke screens distracted the students from moving.

 **Obstacle**

Identifying smoke screens

 **Solutions**

- Many students said they didn't want to sit on the floor because they didn't want to get dirty. I wondered whether dirt was the real reason for their resistance or whether they had learned that chairs, not the floor, were proper and adultlike places to sit.
- Students wore shoes that were unsafe for dance (dress shoes with slick soles or platform or high-heeled shoes). I couldn't ask them to remove their shoes because dancing in bare feet on tile flooring over concrete would have presented other safety issues. Girls insisted on wearing dresses that exposed underwear while dancing or long, narrow skirts that limited leg movements.
- Students heard and responded to rock or soul music by jumping around as if they were playing a guitar or mimicking Michael Jackson. Their movements did not relate to the beat of the music and did not display any connection between the body and mind. When other styles of music (waltz, blues, Celtic, swing) were played, there was little movement response.
- Many kindergarten through fifth-grade students had few dance experiences. In physical education and music classes, they learned reel and square dances and were able to perform choreographed unison movement. But in their personal lives, dancing and dance influences were limited. It appeared that a few girls in each school had seen the *Nutcracker* and other classical ballets. Only about 5 percent of the students took classes in dance studios. There was some interest in country line dancing and aerobics, which were part of pop culture and brought an awareness of dance to the community.

 Tip

Be aware of your students' reactions to you. Are they with you or is there resistance?

 **Trench Truth**

The smoke screens described are examples from my experience in a unique location; your experience may be totally different. The point is that if the students resist participating in dance classes, you should investigate the situation. Be as objective as you can be. You may need to step back and let them show you who they are and what they can do in relation to dance. People have been dancing for thousands of years, and how your students move or don't move has value. Try not to judge their ideas of dance in relation to yours.

Ya Gotta Know the Territory

Making the critical observations necessary to identify smoke screens led me to further investigate the community where I was teaching: How did religion affect people's movements? How did students from various socioeconomic levels move? Did gender influence how people danced? Were ethnic differences a factor in relation to creative dance? Identifying the cultural themes within the community and the obstacles to dance was essential to addressing the problems I encountered in the dance class. This information will not be the same in all parts of the country, but I use my specific situation as a research guide to help you identify some of the factors that may influence your dance program.

 **Obstacle**

Understanding a way of life

 **Solution**

In the Northwest community where I taught, there was a mishmash of cultures. The city was relatively young, and although remnants of Native American and early European American settlers existed, the area was home to people from many cultures loosely connected to their roots. The city was expanding as a suburb; and I began to accept that a suburban lifestyle was a legitimate culture although, unlike most cultures, it wasn't hundreds of years old nor was it about ethnicity. This culture was a community of somewhat disconnected people who lived in the same vicinity and worked a similar five-day week. They went to the mall, enjoyed watching videotapes, surfed the Internet, and carted their children to and from ball games and to an assortment of classes in the private sector. The rains affected the lifestyle in the Northwest, but many people appeared to enjoy the peace and the natural beauty of the environment.

 Tip

Know the community. Examine yourself and what you have to offer in relationship to them. Analyze the situation.

Trench Truth

Things are not always as they appear to be. Before you start teaching, talk with the principal and other faculty members about the community, its values, and its expectations for education. Ask about the students and their families. Read the paper, visit the local diner, talk to people in the neighborhood, and investigate people's preferred styles of entertainment. Even if you are teaching across town from your home, know that cultural differences may exist between the community where you live and the one where you teach.

In God We Trust

Freedom of religion is one of our rights as Americans. However, in the public school environment it is difficult to acknowledge the beliefs of one religious group without ignoring those of another. It is also difficult to work with very young children who are caught between honoring the values of their parents and understanding or accepting the values of another religious group.

 **Obstacle**

Identifying religious beliefs

 **Solutions**

- The community tended to be conservative about dance and pop culture. The Christian fundamentalist churches in the area prohibited dancing, and children from those churches were not able to participate in the creative movement classes. Children were caught between moving creatively and adhering to their religious values. Many parents visited dance classes to assess whether creative movement was actually dance. Some insisted that their children be excluded from the classes, while others could see that creative movement did not represent their view of dance.
- Most parents did not permit their children to watch music television (MTV®) because of videos containing sensual movement and sexual language. When the students saw videos of dancers in leotards moving their hips or embracing each other, they covered their eyes or groaned.
- In the schools where I taught there was a strong population of Jehovah's Witnesses. These children were able to participate in dance class but they were not able to celebrate holidays or participate in performance themes of celebration.
- There were Hindu and Buddhist populations in the schools, but religion did not appear to influence their participation in dance classes.

Tip

Be aware that the belief systems of the people will affect their level of participation in dance classes.

 **Trench Truth**

One year a first-grade teacher told me that her class was studying the Chinese New Year. She wanted me to do the dragon dance or something related to it in the dance class. I started the class with a children's book on the Chinese New Year. I thought I would encourage the students to create movements accordingly. Two students started crying and said that they were not to celebrate anything. A third student was hysterical because in his culture they celebrated the lion, not the dragon. I hadn't mentioned any type of movement at that time, but these three children were so upset that I let them sit and watch. They sat with their fingers in their ears so that they wouldn't hear anything. At that time, I decided to do my own version of Chinese movement and called the dance "The Lanterns." I directed the children in a series of walking and swinging movements. When the children sitting on the side saw what we were doing, they asked to participate because it would be all right with their parents.

In a teaching situation, you need to be aware of the students' responses and react to them appropriately. Very young children should not be challenged to make decisions about religious beliefs that are opposed to the teachings of their families.

Gender Differences

Currently brain researchers are investigating differences in the way men and women think. In the creative dance class it is apparent, generally speaking, that boys and girls process information differently.

 **Obstacle**

Learning gender expectations

 **Solutions**

- Gender differences were obvious in the processing of information and in implied expectations. Gender guidelines for movement were established long before the students started school. The boys were expected to be active and creative, but the girls were expected to be quiet and compatible. Although dance had the reputation of being "an activity for sissies," the boys enjoyed the opportunity for physical risk taking. The girls appeared physically restricted and did not venture into creativity. These goals and reactions affected dance class. The girls needed a lot of encouragement and had to be coaxed into taking risks and thinking "outside the box."
- Most students, regardless of grade level, opposed partnering with the opposite sex. Even the younger students argued or poked fun at one another when working with the opposite sex.
- Puberty and the anticipation of puberty were the death of dance in fifth grade. The students were able to move but the psychological awareness of their bodies inhibited their movements.

Tip

Think about your views of gender differences in relation to dance. Be open to the students' responses when you ask them to perform certain movements.

Trench Truth

The fifth-grade students were taught a course called Growth and Human Development. The information in this course was important, but learning it affected the way students moved. For many students the new awareness of what was happening (or was going to happen) to their bodies was overwhelming. They literally came to an immediate standstill. Getting them to move their arms was a major accomplishment. Once a fifth-grade teacher told the boys that they would not be able to control themselves because they had "raging hormones." Well, they raged for the rest of the school year.

Does Socioeconomic Class Matter?

To teach effectively, you will need to alter your teaching style according to your students' various socioeconomic classes. Each class has its strengths and weaknesses and its good characteristics and problems.

 **Obstacle**

Recognizing socioeconomic levels

 **Solutions**

- When I arrived in the Northwest, I investigated the history. The city's population was predominantly Caucasians who ranged from middle to high socioeconomic status. Between 1990 and 2000 there was a population influx that radically changed the school population. Low-income housing, homeless shelters, and trailer courts in the area provided refuge for many transient families. More than 45 percent of enrolled students represented a low socioeconomic background.

- The change in demographics brought a dramatic change in the needs of the students. Nearly 70 percent of them qualified for special services such as the Title I Learning Assistance Program (LAP), Learning Support Program, English as a Second Language (ESL), and Structured Learning.

- The new demographics, the job market, poverty, a transient way of life, and the social problems of the times brought with them behavioral changes in the students.

- The students from high socioeconomic backgrounds also had their difficulties. Some parents and teachers expected greater success from these students; some parents expected more challenge from their schools. These expectations created stress for many students. Some students had attitudes of superiority toward teachers, school rules, and their classmates.

Tip

The students in each socioeconomic level have experiences from which to draw. Creative dance should reflect who the dancers are or wish to be. Let the work evolve from their experiences.

 **Trench Truth**

A difficult aspect of working with students from a variety of socioeconomic backgrounds in the same class is finding a method of teaching that will work for all of them. The students' intelligence and experiences are not the problem; the difficulty is in the manner of accomplishing work, the style of focus, and the ability to work with others. For example, generally speaking, students with middle-to-high socioeconomic backgrounds are more focused and take pride in accomplishing works. Students in low socioeconomic levels are plagued by problems and expectations that affect their ability to focus and to achieve high goals. These characteristics also affect the way the groups interrelate.

Ethnic Diversity

The United States is an experiment in honoring diversity. It is the first country in history where people of different cultures, different religions, different values, and different languages officially live together with one goal: the pursuit of happiness.

 **Obstacle**

Acknowledging ethnicity

 **Solutions**

- Many people were flocking to the Northwest from California, Idaho, and Oregon; and a population of Russian and Mexican immigrants speaking English as a second language was also growing. The student population remained predominantly (about 85 percent) Caucasian.

- About 5 percent of the students were African American. In the dance class these students exhibited little movement to any style of music. If I related to them through dance, they froze. From discussions with the students and parents, I realized that the African American students were trying to fit into this predominantly Caucasian population and didn't want to be singled out, especially in the area of dance.

- The Russians, who were recent immigrants to the United States, had come to this country to escape religious persecution. They were sponsored by Christian fundamentalist churches that were extremely strict in their beliefs and customs, especially in regard to dance. Aware of their reasons for immigration, the school administrators worked with their church authorities to compare creative movement and physical education. The parents visited the creative movement classes. After several years of discussion, most children were allowed to participate.

- The Asian and Hispanic students were the most open to the creative movement experience. The Asian students appeared to enjoy the opportunity to create, and they worked tirelessly on perfecting their dance projects. The Hispanic students, many of whom were shy, moved freely to music, learned quickly, and demonstrated a cultural connection to dance.

Tip

Understand the population by identifying similarities in socioeconomic background, ethnicity, gender, and religion. Before proceeding to the teaching arena, note how these factors relate to you and your cultural experiences. Then teach with respect for similarities and differences.

 **Trench Truth**

Views of poverty have changed over the years. During the Great Depression of the 1930s, people who were poor or destitute struggled financially but were able to maintain personal dignity. During the 1960s, many people rejected American bureaucracy, and being poor was associated with anti-establishment values. It was the trend for the hippie generation. But in the 1990s, poverty was often associated with drug use, alcoholism, laziness, immoral lifestyles, and imprisonment. This stereotype still exists and it colors the views of administrators, teachers, and the community. Be on guard for an erroneous poverty equation.

Getting Started

During my first year in the Northwest, I introduced a creative dance program in two schools. The program was designed to take students into new areas of thought, movement, imagination, and feeling. I was responsible for teaching five or six classes at each grade level (kindergarten through fifth grade), which meant I taught about 30 to 32 classes per week and worked with each classroom teacher. Establishing working relationships with classroom teachers is essential because they are the link to the students and parents.

 ## Obstacle

Bringing the classroom teachers on board

 ## Solutions

- During the teacher work days, or inservice days, I met with teachers from each grade level to explain the creative dance program. I placed great emphasis on the thinking aspects of dance and how these would relate to thinking skills used in reading and math. I explained the movement skills and how these related to brain development.

- I explained the new arts program. The school district was attempting to place the arts (dance, music, and visual arts) in a weekly two-hour block of time. The arts block served as a planning time for classroom teachers. The concept of the block promoted arts integration. The arts teachers could collaborate on developing connections of arts elements and concepts, such as rhythm, value, and line.

- The arts schedule, which needed to correlate with space concerns, lunch and recess times, and other programs in the school, was established with the principal.

- Unfortunately, we did not discuss class management during the first meeting. This was a huge mistake, and it took me a while to establish the support of the classroom teachers for my class management techniques (see chapter 3).

Tip

Establish a positive relationship with the classroom teachers. Be clear about your goals, your expectations, and the possibility of working on projects together.

Trench Truth

It was the class from hell, led by Lucifer himself. A group of extremely tough-looking fifth graders had their first experience with creative dance class. Levels, directions, and energies did not impress them. Their goals were to mock every idea that was introduced, to laugh at one another's movements, and to have as much aggressive physical contact as possible. My approach was to take one day at a time and experiment with a variety of movements that might capture their interest.

A behavioral reporting plan was established with the classroom teachers. Although the arts teachers took care of immediate behavior problems, a class chart was used to report behavior that was extremely out of line. The teachers agreed to monitor this reporting tool along with behavior plans that many students had in the classroom.

On several occasions I had reported outrageous behavior to Lucifer, the teacher of the class from hell. Even after I had discussed the students' inappropriate behavior with this teacher, I never noticed a change in behavior, which in many cases was motivated by the classroom teacher. My course of action then was to work with the students on their behavior plans during recess.

For the following class period, the teacher did not escort the entire class to the gym but sent them as they each completed their classroom assignments. They chaotically entered—creeping, walking, running, or stopping to play in small groups in the schoolyard. After several students were in the gym, a group started fighting outside. I walked out to attend to those students as others ran in. When I got back to the gym, several students were dribbling basketballs, others were running through the space, and three had climbed on tall cabinets and proceeded to walk on a small ledge at the top of the wall. I gathered the students who were able to hear me and we sat in the center of the gym. We sat in silence. When the others realized that I was not going to chase them around the room or scream at them, they slowly began to sit down near the group.

A classroom party was set for the afternoon. So I planned to use deprivation of the entire party or a portion of the party as the consequence for the students' behavior. I simply said, "The following students are to report to the gym at two o'clock: . . ." Then I taught the class.

I sent a note to the teacher describing the situation and notified the principal of my plan. Two o'clock came and no students arrived. I had the secretary call the teacher to see whether the students were on their way. I never received an answer. So I headed to the classroom and found the party in full swing. Lucifer asked what I wanted and said that he had gotten the note but didn't understand the situation. Then he called the students in question. In front of the students he said to me, "Now I'd like to hear both sides of the story before I will agree to have these students miss the party." He undermined my authority in front of the students, which alerted me to the reason I was having so much difficulty with this class. But determinedly I said, "You have nothing to say and no judgment to give in this situation." I took the students back to the gym as he yelled out to me, "How long will you keep them?"

The rest of the year was a battle with this teacher and unfortunately the principal did not take a stand. The students, however, learned that I was going to follow through with the consequences, in spite of their classroom teacher's lack of cooperation.

Moving the Students

In many communities in which dance is integral to the culture, students come into public education with skills and knowledge of dance, with established dance aesthetics, and with a perception of personal identity and dance heritage. But in this public school community, dance was a relatively new concept. I was truly oblivious of my lack of awareness about this community. Although I thought I was prepared, my personal education was just beginning.

 **Obstacle**

Bringing kids on board

 **Solutions**

- Many students entered the class with great apprehension about this new experience. Many hid their fears with rowdy, silly, or resistant behavior. Their views of dance were set and were quite negative. During my first meeting with each class, I briefly talked about the privilege of the arts program that was offered to them. The students looked at me as if I had lost my mind. I received their feedback with great interest. The older students were angry because they wanted to play ball; the younger students were skeptical about the possibility of partner dancing; and some younger girls anticipated becoming ballerinas, while some boys feared they would have to wear dance tights. Most were afraid that they would feel and look foolish. I explained what creative dance is and how the class would function:

  > Creative dance isn't ballet, tap, jazz, hip-hop, square dance, or social dance, although we may choose to do some of these dance forms. Creative dance is movement that expresses an idea. You will explore movement about particular themes such as running, jumping, and turning. Then, you will put your movements together to create dances. You will be working with a partner or a small group. It will be your movement, your ideas, and your dance. I will set the structure.

- Most of the students appeared to listen and were willing to give it a try. Nevertheless, the creative dance experience, which requires them to move, was frightening and overwhelming for many students.

- As I attempted to establish relaxed but focused movement classes, I encouraged and praised the students for the slightest movement and allowed them to giggle over the silliest things. The pace of the class was relatively quick, which I hoped would raise their energy level and get them moving without giving it too much thought. However, the students were so self-conscious they could barely move or think of a movement. Many students asked to sit out or go to the bathroom.

- It was a struggle to get the fourth and fifth graders to cooperate. They soaked up an extreme amount of my energy while I was continually coaxing, prodding, encouraging, and addressing disciplinary concerns. I needed to be aware of everything that was happening in the class while maintaining a balance between understanding their needs and moving them to a different plane. Providing these students with activities that gave them positive dance experiences and fostered a gentle change of view required much patience and stamina.

 Tip

Put your energies where you have the most success. The program will grow with those students and will influence the others in the school. If you only focus on the failures, you will likely give up. Prepare your strategy. Control and focus the troops. Know your goals and your methods of attack. Be on guard!

Trench Truth

Imagine an elementary school gym as 30 fifth graders enter the space, many of whom tower over me. As the door closes the classroom teacher calls out, "Have fun." The kids freely run into the space, and for some reason they associate screaming with fun. The energy is unceasing, and as one settles down another bursts into explosive behavior. Yet, it is the contrast of controlled energy that makes the dance and the teaching of dance exquisite. But I'm not fooled—I prepare myself for combat!

Sometimes, I feel as if I am in a war zone. My insides are frenzied; a state of panic looms over me; my vocal cords tighten; and I'd like to

tie and gag each one of those darling children (but that's not politically correct). How will I get the class under control? What procedures am I expecting them to follow? Without crushing their spirits, how will I animate the meek while centering the rest? How will I channel this incredible energy into creative dance? Little by little I allow them to see that I am firm and gentle, not schizophrenic.

Establishing Class Rules

The Rules

Before the school year begins consider how to establish a safe and nurturing learning environment for your students. Yes, the children will be cute; but don't base class orderliness and a focused learning environment on how darling and how much fun the children will be. These precious darlings are waiting like hawks to seize the moment and are ready to challenge you to see how far they can go. They desperately seek to know where the boundaries are. Appropriate behavior requires thinking, participating, and communicating while each student demonstrates behavior that is respectful to herself and others. Within these boundaries, spontaneity is highly valued.

 **Obstacle**

Organizing the rules

 **Solutions**

- Consider the rules that will guide the class. There should be only two or three rules that are very broad. These rules will serve as an umbrella under which most behaviors can be placed. All the other dos and don'ts should be class procedures.
- In my classes, behaviors are categorized into two general rules: (1) Be good to yourself and (2) respect others. These rules are intended to discourage movements, gestures, and responses that would harm or offend children in the class. In almost every class, some aspect of the rules is introduced, reiterated, or enforced.

 Tip

Make the rules broad and simple, and test kids on rules in relationship to everything they do.

Trench Truth

In a school where I taught, the teachers determined that the children didn't follow the rules simply because they didn't know them. The teachers met in teams and decided on what they didn't want the children to do in the school and at recess. They wrote, laminated, and posted beautiful signs displaying the rules. Most of the signs positively addressed the requirements. The rules were posted on the walls of every room and hallway. However, some of the children were unable to read the signs. Others did not remember to look at them. Another method of dealing with the situation was to put graffiti on them and eventually rip them off the walls.

Rule 1: Be Good to Yourself

The concept of being good to oneself seems outside the realm of possibility for many children. Most students are unaware that they are able to be good to themselves. Discussions about positive and negative actions and their results should be extensive.

 **Obstacle**

Injuring themselves

 **Solutions**

- Discuss physical dangers (such as sliding across the floor and crashing into the wall) that appear to be favorite pastimes, especially for boys. Actually, there's nothing wrong with either of these actions. Yet, when 30 students are doing these actions indiscriminately, danger is imminent. If someone gets hurt, the teacher is responsible. In my most dramatic manner, I relate the following examples when appropriate.

  I know you really enjoy crashing into the wall, especially when it has a soft mat against it. Last year a large fifth-grade boy was running to bounce off the wall, but when he was about 4 feet from the wall he tripped. He did a belly flop, his head bounced off the wall, and he landed on his face. Blood was gushing from his mouth and nose. The nurse came to his rescue and his mom rushed him to the dentist. It was very sad, because he knocked out his permanent front tooth. I don't want that to happen to you, nor do I want to be responsible if that happens to you because I will feel very sad. So, please, please, *please* be good to yourself and make wise choices with your movements.

  Sliding across the room is really fun, isn't it? I know that you like to do it, but it can be very dangerous. A couple of years ago in another school, there was a kid who always slid across the room. No matter how many times I asked him to stop, he ignored me. One day he came running into the gym and attempted to slide on his side. He was going so fast that he slid, hit the side of his head, and flipped over on his back. The whole class heard his head bounce two times on the floor. Did he cry, you ask? First of all, he was almost knocked unconscious. When he felt the pain, he screamed and cried. He was

sent to the first-aid room, where he remained until the end of the school day. He had two huge bumps on his head and a very, very bad headache. He was lucky he didn't get a concussion. I don't want that to happen to you, nor do I want to be responsible if that happens to you because I will be very sad. So, please, please, *please* be good to yourself and make wise choices with your movements

- Physical danger is not the only aspect of the rule. When students are good to themselves, they develop strong self-management skills and positive self-concepts, enhance their ability to focus on assignments, and acquire positive reputations that follow them throughout their lives:

Another way to be good to yourself is to think about your actions and how they will affect others. If your actions are positive and good for others, they will be good for you. If your actions distract others from learning or bring harm to them, they will also get you into trouble, and then you won't be good to yourself. Can anyone tell me some ways in which you can be good to yourself? (Discuss.) Can anyone tell me ways in which you will not be good to yourself? (Discuss.) Here's an example: If you continuously distract others during the class, they will be unable to learn and they will be unhappy with you. Even if you're just trying to be funny, others will quickly decide that they do not want to work with you. You will end up with a bad reputation and lose a lot of friends. You will not be good to yourself and there will be consequences for your actions.

Tip

Emphasize and reemphasize rules of safety to the children. Their safety is your responsibility.

Trench Truth

Children respond positively to stories. Stories can be nonconfrontational and can have specific examples of behaviors that you are trying to teach. Children will get the point, share the story with others, and remind their classmates of the story when an occasion requires it.

Rule 2: Respect Others

Respect emerges as a response or anticipation to interaction. The manner in which society shows respect changes over time. Students need to be taught the standards of respect that are required in the dance class.

 **Obstacle**

Poking, hitting, slapping

 **Solutions**

- In my early years of developing the dance program, a major problem for children was learning to move freely. Many students focused on hitting, poking, punching, slapping, and tripping others. Dance movement was not their intention. Others felt awkward and uncomfortable about moving and about having others see them move. It appeared that laughing at each other was a natural response, and it only exacerbated the problem.

- The rule *respect others* prohibits disrespectful behaviors. When a student exhibits inappropriate behaviors, I stop the class. We discuss the observation and how these behaviors are not respectful of others. You can discuss most observations without naming or pointing a finger at the students who were responsible. For example:

  I just noticed that someone poked another while skipping past. Let's keep our hands in our own personal bubble while skipping.

- A private discussion with the student(s) who engaged in the behavior is a good approach. I usually ask the student(s) to describe what happened, why they demonstrated that behavior, and why it was disrespectful to others. We usually discuss it on a one-to-one or small-group basis, depending on the number of students involved. Then we discuss the consequence that may or may not be necessary.

- Many students who are nervous about dancing do not understand dance. Consequently, they may laugh or make fun of other kids' movement. This behavior is disrespectful. When the students are the audience, they should be allowed to laugh only if the dance is intended to be a comedy.

  If you respect others, you will encourage them to do good work and help them to feel comfortable when they are dancing. If you laugh at someone, he will feel really bad and may never dance again. If you whisper or laugh while someone is dancing, it distracts the dancer and other audience members. The dancer begins to think that the audience is making fun of her, and she will feel embarrassed. Therefore, laughing at each other is prohibited. Remember that if you respect your classmates, they will respect you when it is your turn to dance.

Tip

For four or five class periods, the rules may be the focus while moving. Once the students demonstrate that they understand the rules and consequences, the class moves smoothly throughout the year, and these rules need only be reviewed on rare occasions.

Trench Truth

There is no method of discipline that can be proven as tried and true. The situation changes with each child, each class, and each school. Although dance is a kinesthetic art form, I *try not* to touch a child, especially in anger or as a consequence to a negative action. I cannot predict the child's interpretation of the touch. If I need to make physical contact, I ask the child's permission (i.e., "Do you mind if I touch your shoulder?").

In my classes, when one child behaves badly, the entire class could be disrupted, so I have to consider the rest of the class when reacting to the behavior. My decision of whether to call out the child's name varies according to the child, the number of times he has disturbed the class, and the seriousness of the situation. My concern for embarrassing a child is not in calling out the child's name but in my tone of voice. In most cases, when a child is confronted in front of the class, she has already embarrassed herself through her behavior. When a situation is serious enough for me to acknowledge a child's inappropriate behavior in front of the class, I need to resolve the behavior, at times by discussing the situation with the child and the rest of the class. Apologies may be in order, and consequences will probably follow. These situations are rare occasions, but they do happen.

Respecting Partners

The concept of respect is most challenging when students begin working with partners. Working with others is a required life skill, and in creative dance class I emphasize respecting and working with others.

 **Obstacle**

Hurting other people's feelings

 **Solutions**

- I assign partners so the children learn to work with many different classmates, not just their friends. Some children may initially respond by making faces, rolling their eyes, sticking out their tongues, crying, throwing tantrums, or refusing to work with the assigned partners. Others may giggle or poke fun at the student who is in a boy–girl pair or with the child everyone considers the loser of the class. I usually address these problems with the class by dramatizing how the behaviors appear to the discriminated

student: A popular boy is prompted to ask me to be his partner. As soon as he asks, I respond by making a sour face, abruptly turning my back to him, and grunting, "No!" The response usually shocks the class, yet they appear to understand the point. We discuss how the boy felt, and I illicit from the students other feelings that they had experienced at that time or at another time in their lives. (I don't choose a girl for this demonstration because, in my experience, many girls take it seriously, cry, or never forgive me.)

- When dances require students to touch others' hands, many students exhibit discrimination by refusing to hold hands, pulling their shirt sleeves over their hands to avoid touching, or refusing to face a particular student. I enforce the *respect others* policy. At times, I notice students sitting stoned-faced rather than responding negatively—a reaction to avoid the consequences. Although students do not embrace the idea of working with people they don't particularly like, they learn that toleration is a small step toward respect. My objective is that students will eventually learn to understand and respect the strengths and limitations of others.

Tip

As time progresses, partnering with many different classmates becomes an expected standard. To persuade the students to choose or be chosen by a variety of partners, I use humor by saying, "You are only working with your partner for a short time; you are not marrying that person!"

Trench Truth

During the early months of the program, it seemed as if I was constantly stopping the class to acknowledge behavior: "Megan and Yara, pushing does not show respect for others." "Chris and Trevor, I like the way you were showing respect for others by passing each other without bumping." "Ben, I like the way you gently lifted your partner." By midyear, inappropriate behaviors were minimized. The need to constantly monitor behavior subsided and the students were able to focus on dance. It appeared that the students knew the expectations and had changed their behaviors. As time progressed, some students created dances about their anger or their desire to disrupt the class. This type of self-expression is acceptable because it has form and order. In a few years, it became rare for any student (except those new to the school) to engage in inappropriate or disrespectful behaviors.

Managing Your Class

Give Me That Old-Time Religion

My first year on the job was an eye-opener. Some classes accepted the program and began to experience dance. However, in other classes the pendulum swung wildly as many fourth and fifth graders tested, tried, and taunted the structure of the class.

The students . . .
> bumped,
>> tripped,
>>> pushed,
>>>> punched,
>>>>> yelled,
>>>>>> argued,
>>>>>>> climbed the walls,
>>>>>>>> ran uncontrollably,
>>>>>>>>> and crawled onto the rafters.

It was the first time in my career that I experienced moments when I couldn't get 10- and 11-year-old children under control. I tried the tricks that had proven successful in other situations. But for some of these classes, nothing appeared to work.

My approach for teaching creative dance is opposed to control and suppression. I prefer a class in which the students are relaxed yet focused, enjoying themselves yet learning. I envisioned the students walking into the class, sitting or lying down to discuss the class activities, doing a dance warm-up, and then working cooperatively in small groups to create dances. But during the first year of the program, it didn't work that way.

In the early years of developing the program, class management began with the most extreme basic training. For example, the students didn't have a concept of the word *walk*. They ran into the space and tested their sliding abilities, hoping to arrive close to the designated place. Lying down provided the students a time for drifting or for distracting others. Sitting was difficult, but it offered a better chance for focus. Many students wanted to sit on the stage or on the stage steps, which seemed to be a reasonable idea. But I found them rolling under the curtains, hiding in the wings for the entire class period, crawling under the steps, and having private conversations during instructions and class discussions. None of these ideas are extreme if the students are ready to dance and are eager to be in the class. But the students I encountered my first year were not ready to handle the anticipated freedoms. I had to establish a positive attitude about dance, and I had to teach the students the responsibilities of freedom.

 **Obstacle**

Getting students under control

 **Solutions**

- I drew on some of the methods of class management that I learned during my student-teaching days in parochial schools. I set clear expectations for behavior, established boundaries, and enforced consequences. These methods helped me structure creative dance classes and maintain my sanity.

- Early in the school year, I awakened students to the physical boundaries, acceptable behavior, and consequences for both positive and negative actions. Rules and consequences cannot stand alone; when combined with positive reinforcement, explanation, and discussion, they can be effective.

- Children feel secure when they know the parameters in which they will work. Boundaries keep them from testing the waters to see how far they are allowed to go before they are stopped or before the teacher shows concern for them. This type of structure and order does not limit creativity; rather, it provides a safe environment in which the whole class is able to create (see Consequences, pages 49 through 53).

 ## Tip

From the minute they walk into the room, students will test you. If you allow them too much freedom at the beginning of the year, you will be at their mercy. Teach the rules and enforce them immediately and consistently. Yes, they are darling, sweet children, but many are manipulative or have troubled lives and emotional difficulties that they express with inappropriate behavior. If you do not establish boundaries and consequences, the year will be unbearable and *you* will have emotional difficulties!

Trench Truth

For whatever it's worth, I did my student teaching in a Catholic school where the students were disciplined and controlled the "old-fashioned" way. My teaching supervisor, Sister Mary Estelle Foucheaux, MSC, impressed on me that the climate of the class, set in the first six weeks of school, will determine the attitude and environment of the class for the rest of the year. She jokingly told me, "Don't smile until December. The students are sizing you up and testing you to see how far they are permitted to go. If they are uncontrollable in September, April and May will be unbearable." Her idea was to take control of the students and then gently relax as the year progressed: Keep the bit in their mouths and release it when they are ready; if not, they will run like wild horses, dragging you behind them.

After six years and a variety of schools, I was able to loosen the reins. I don't have to be on guard every minute. I established the standards for the classes, and by some form of osmosis the incoming students knew the expectations and goals for the class.

Praise and Correction

Many philosophies about praise and correction of behavior exist, and it's best to know the thinking of the administration and the faculty at the beginning of your teaching experience. If the basic beliefs for praise and correction are not the same among the administration and faculty, teaching and receiving support for your style of class management will be perplexing. Praise and correction are partners in developing self-esteem, and you need to use both for managing your class—5 or 10 praises for every correction!

 **Obstacle**

Balancing praise and correction

 ## Solutions

- Once the students are aware of their boundaries and know what constitutes appropriate behavior, I praise them when they demonstrate these behaviors. For example:

  "I like the way Sam and John are working as a team." "Wow! Everyone, please notice how Kevin and Mark can move through the space without crashing into each other." "Logan and Tyson, could you demonstrate how you move backward? Notice how they look over their shoulders so as not to bump into each other."

- I use a lot of "I" statements when speaking to the class because they suggest my reaction to the behavior. The student is not accused but is gently reminded of respectful behaviors. For example:

  "I am really pleased with the way you entered the dance space today." "I am unhappy about your lack of attention while I was giving instructions." "I am very happy about your focus today." "Boys and girls, I am so disappointed about the way you performed your warm-up. I know that you can do so much better. Let's try it again." "The noise level is really bothering me and I can't hear what others are asking."

- When young children receive praise, they respond accordingly. As students grow older, they want to hear praise but they also want it to be genuine. When focusing on praise, I try to be clear about the degree of praise that is earned, such as:

  "I liked the way you *tried* to work in the group." "Your movement was *good;* however, I wonder if you could do the same movement without screaming." "The way you worked as a team was *great.*" "Your dance focus was *excellent,* even as visitors were walking through the room." "This class is *so fantastic* that I really enjoy working with you."

- I give students praise when they have earned it. Some children hear comments of praise so much that the phrases become meaningless. They are able to detect insincere praise, and they also know that no one is consistently good. Continuous superlative praise tends to lower the standards and goals for the class. Children begin to rationalize that if they are so wonderful, why try to be better?

- My reward system is usually intrinsic. The students receive verbal praise and recognition in the class; they become aware that they are respected and trusted; they are selected for special jobs such as erasing the board, delivering a message, or giving out the pencils.
- So often a child develops a troublesome reputation, and everything that the child does supports the problem. Often, I must overlook inappropriate behavior and place emphasis on good behavior—no matter how insignificant. For example, "John, you are standing so tall today," or "Chris, I really like the way you walked to your place." Making a positive comment about one particular behavior could change a student's general behavior in the class; once praised, the student may reduce her bad behavior and begin to focus on contributing rather than disrupting the class.

Tip

Begin each class with an open mind. It provides a fresh start for every student.

Trench Truth

In the early years of the arts program, I noticed that the children were rewarded with candy for performing well. I thought that maybe I should do the same. I tried it a few times, and it didn't feel right to me. I discussed it with my students, who believed that a performer gets paid and that the candy was their payment. That's true, but in the arts it takes years, if ever, to reach the monetary reward. So I devised another approach. I began to play up the applause factor during teaching and rehearsal. I also told the students that the reward would come when they took their bow and that they had to take a slow bow to hear the reward. I wanted them to feel accomplishment, pride, and appreciation. The day after a performance I visited each class who had performed so that I could give my praises and share the special comments that I had received about them. A few students shared their feelings about their parents' responses or their own personal thoughts. I concluded the visit by saying, "You achieved your goal and have received your reward. Congratulations!" It appeared that they began to understand that rewards do not always have to be tangible.

Educational Views on Praise and Correction

Current education places enormous emphasis on self-esteem. The questions are these: What is self-esteem? Is it based on praise? Achievement? Reality? Personal control? Stability? A sense of who one is? The answer to all these questions is yes. And where is self-esteem developed? In these family? School? During the first six months of life?

The school's teachers and administrators should be responsible for building a trusting relationship with each child and for providing a secure, stable environment that promotes self-esteem. The environment should be a place where each student becomes aware of his strengths and weaknesses, where students are challenged and encouraged, and where they are able to grow. In this environment, each child will have an idea of reality—his achievements, mistakes, and potential. The students will be able to appreciate who they are and realize what they hope to achieve.

 **Obstacle**

Deciding on the best approach to praise and correction

 Solutions

- Current thinking in education places emphasis on praise and gentle correction. This approach promotes speaking in a calm, caring tone and offering the child time to explain the problems that arise. The teacher listens and compares the child's explanation to other experiences the child has had in order to understand the reason for any inappropriate behavior. A caring environment is preferred for teaching, and in this environment students should feel comfortable to communicate any problems they may have that affect their behavior. But should inappropriate behavior be excused during every class because of "normally dysfunctional" homes and lives?

- Compassion for a child and the situation in which he lives is necessary. But compassion should not be confused with pity. A compassionate teacher offers concern for the child and a desire to help the child reach his potential. Pity, on the other hand, encourages a child to develop "poor me syndrome." Excusing behavior because of pity encourages the child to become a prisoner of the past, and the child will continue to find excuses not to grow.

- Another thought in education is that correction should be private; a child should not be embarrassed or humiliated in front of the class. Embarrassment puts the child's self-esteem at risk. Humiliation affects self-esteem; but if a child has disrupted the class, should the correction be a class issue? The other students wait to see whether their classmate will get away with inappropriate behavior. It is, however, an injustice to the class if the teacher does not take the time or the energy to correct inappropriate behavior—the manner of correction depends on the situation. When the problem is not observable by the others or when only a few children are involved, you can correct students quietly and privately. The method will vary according to the situation and according to the culture. In some cultures children would be mortified if corrected or even if their names were said aloud; in other cultures, a snappy response to a snappy behavior is part of the game.

 Tip

In using praise and correction, be specific and provide information that is educational. When offering students both praise and correction you give them the opportunity to increase knowledge, grow in personal control, have a perspective of reality, and enhance self-esteem.

 Trench Truth

I've worked in elementary schools where the philosophy of the school and the parents placed emphasis on the idea that school is fun. The school schedule was set up accordingly: Activities, play days, and funny dress-up days were daily or weekly experiences. The aim was to protect the children from stress, from challenging and uncomfortable experiences, and from imposed order. But the students were continuously distracted from the content of the material. Faculty and parents questioned the style of creative dance classes, which maintained structure and order and had a challenging creative format. They also disregarded the concept that change and growth require some pain and hard work. As a result, the students who were very talented were never challenged to their full potential.

Dance Class Management System

The school district designed a new report card that provided a space for two dance grades: demonstration of concepts and processes of dance, and participation and cooperation. Comment forms that accompany the report card were also available.

To respond to the new report cards, JoAnn Amberg, a physical education and dance educator in Enumclaw, Washington, suggested the following method that brought extraordinary behavior results. The method was a system designed to help students become independent self-managers and to take responsibility for their actions. I introduced the new self-management chart to the students in relation to the new report card. I explained the rubrics to the students. At the end of each class, they gathered to score themselves according to the first behavior rubric that follows.

 **Obstacle**

Establishing a behavior rubric

 **Solutions**

- This first plan was used as a trial method to see whether the concept worked. The students scored themselves with a plus, check, or minus according to these criteria:

    Plus (+) = Made wise choices and decisions; focused on the task; respected others and worked cooperatively.

    Check (√) = Made good choices when reminded; focused on the task when the teacher was watching; visited and distracted others.

    Minus (−) = Made poor choices; was not focused on the task; interfered with others' learning.

- The students gathered for scoring at the end of class. As I called their names, they responded with their scores. Occasionally, if I disagreed with a student's score, I either reminded the student of his demonstrated behavior during class or I raised my eyebrows awaiting a different response. Many children forgot their inappropriate behavior from early in the class and needed to be gently reminded. However, if a child thought that she gave herself a fair

score, I was happy to hear the explanation. At times, children commented on an incident that occurred that involved others. This sometimes resulted in a change of score. Many children forgot that the teacher is a person who would like to be treated with respect. When a student was a distraction to the class or disrespectful to me, it was usually addressed during the class. During the scoring, I reminded the students of the following: "The rubric states, 'Respect others,' and I am an 'other.' This may change a score."

- When I started the rubric method the process took about 8 to 10 minutes. This time was extremely important and well worth it. The class was then able to proceed with few behavioral incidents because they knew what was expected of them. After several weeks the time was reduced to about 5 minutes, including the time for gathering, scoring, and saying good-bye. My students looked forward to this activity because for many it brought closure and gave them a time to reflect on their accomplishments.

- Fourth- and fifth-grade students asked to keep the criteria but to use a number system of 5 to 0. If they met three criteria in the plus (+) area, the score was 5 (outstanding); if they met two criteria, the score was 4 (very good). If they met three criteria in the check (√)

area, the score was 3 (good); and if they met two criteria, the score was 2 (not so good). In the minus (–) area, 1 is inappropriate and 0 is a recess time or a visit to the principal.

- Two years later, the management system evolved into one in which students earned 1 point for each of these criteria:

  Respected self = Needed no reminders to behave well; dressed appropriately; did good things for themselves.

  Respected others = Was kind to others; didn't poke, kick, or laugh at others.

  Focused = Thought about the topic of study and worked accordingly.

  Produced quality work = Work met expectations; "quality" means that someone would pay to see it.

  Collaborated with team = While creating movement every team member gave ideas and also tried the ideas of others; there was no boss.

  Contributed to the knowledge of the class = Raised hand and shared information that was important to the class.

- The students responded favorably to a scoring rubric for behavior because they assumed responsibility for their actions, scored themselves according to a set rubric, and demonstrated an awareness of their actions and how these actions affected the rest of the class.

Tip

A good class management system needs to make sense to the students, should help them to assume responsibility for their actions, and must be enforced. Be aware that a good system also needs to remain flexible enough to meet a variety of needs and situations.

Trench Truth

Although I have taught in six schools, only one had a schoolwide management plan. In this particular school, all faculty and staff members were involved in the success and enforcement of the plan at all times. It provided support for all teachers in their efforts to maintain class management.

The emphasis of the plan was to develop student self-management. The plan combined positive reinforcement for good behavior and corrective discipline for teaching good behavior along with natural and planned consequences. The plan used green, yellow, and red indicators in which green signified good self-management, yellow was a warning, and red indicated a continued or serious problem that required parent involvement.

The school management plan included a "Wheel of Solutions" to deal with conflict resolutions; positive reinforcement that offered special incentive awards for good behavior; and corrective discipline such as contacting or scheduling a conference with a parent, giving detention, taking away special privileges, sending the student home for the remainder of the day, referring the student to a Child Study Team, referring the student to outside agencies, and using district and state disciplinary action policies. Although each specialist teacher (art, music, dance, physical education, reading, media) was responsible for managing his own class, indicators of behavior were reported to the classroom teacher. The classroom teacher managed the indicators for each child and applied the positive or corrective discipline when necessary.

Step-by-Step Management Plan

If a school has a schoolwide management plan, it is always best to confer with the principal about the plan and the part you can play to contribute to its success. It is also a good idea to discuss your own class management plan with the principal to ensure that you have administrative support.

You need to establish your class management plan long before the students arrive in the dance class. Be determined to enforce it, but anticipate that the plan will need to be flexible enough to be adapted as circumstances change. What follows is a summary of some of the steps that should be taken before a child receives a consequence for inappropriate behavior.

 **Obstacle**

Establishing the steps that lead up to a consequence

 **Solutions**

- A child receives a gentle reminder about appropriate behavior.
- Occasionally, for children who are classified as attention deficit/ hyperactive disordered (AD/HD), the approach is different. While gently speaking to the child, I may place my hand on the child's shoulder. This technique helps the child become more grounded, center energy, and establish calmness.
- A child may need to be taken aside for a chat about what is causing the behavior. Often, the total situation is unclear to me or to the child. After a discussion, adjustments or a different perspective from the child's or my view may result.
- If inappropriate behavior continues, the student receives a personal warning and a reminder about the consequence.

 Tip

At the beginning of the year, exert great energy toward establishing class management. Be as consistent as possible. It is even a good idea at the beginning to stop the class to explain the details of your management

system. The students will learn the system quickly, and then you can move the focus to dance for the rest of the year.

 **Trench Truth**

When I worked in an 80-percent high-risk school, inappropriate behavior was constant. I noticed that the younger children responded to a hand on the shoulder or a compliment. The older students wanted to see whether I could enforce the management plan; if I could, it meant that I cared. These students spent time with me at recess; some wanted to be heard and others wanted to vent their anger. Whatever their intentions were, the fact that I gave them my time made a great impression on them, and I began to establish a relationship with the very needy students.

Consequences

Consequences are designed to reinforce boundaries and appropriate behavior. Although a consequence may scare some of the good students into controlled or suppressed behavior, it may be one course of action that is necessary for establishing a safe environment for others. The consequence method is designed to teach the students to think before they act and to be aware that disrespectful actions will not be tolerated. Positive and respectful actions are praised and rewarded. Uncontrolled energy is disruptive and frightening to the class. Disruptive students need help in developing positive behaviors either during the dance class or as an ongoing behavioral plan with the classroom teacher, counselor, or principal.

The students learn quickly that I always follow through with the consequences because I do not offer idle threats. When I say there will be a consequence for a specific inappropriate behavior, I always follow through.

 **Obstacle**

Establishing consequences

 **Solutions**

- The first consequence that I use is to deny the student the dance experience. When I have the student's attention, I tell her to go to the wall, or I just point to the wall without saying anything. I call this consequence "The dreaded wall effect," because when a student has to go to the time-out area she knows she will consequently miss part or all of the dance class. In the primary grades students may go to the wall for a 5-minute time-out and are invited to rejoin the class when the time-out is finished. Five minutes is a long time for a young child, and for most students only one time-out is necessary. However, there are a few who return to time-out two or three times during the class. The second time may be for 10 minutes, and if a third incident occurs she does not rejoin the class. As the grade level increases, so too does the time-out period. The older students, who know that I will definitely follow through with consequences, receive one warning; if inappropriate behaviors continue, they go to time-out for the rest of the class.

- A conference with the classroom teacher gives insight into a child's behavior and possible reasons for the inappropriate behavior. The teacher may have similar concerns or may have the child on a behavioral management program.

- A consequence for a seriously inappropriate behavior is to spend recess standing in the dance space. The student is expected to be in the gym for the full recess period. If the child is late, another recess is in order. This is not an everyday occurrence, and most children need only to miss one recess to learn to follow the rules.

- Another method that has worked in remedying constant behavior problems is a phone call or conference with the child's parent or guardian. Because the dance class is so short and only once a week, I prefer to involve the parent or guardian only when the inappropriate behavior becomes continuous. During conversations with parents, a great deal is revealed about the child's family situation, values, and communication. In some cases, the problem in dance class is solved immediately. Other parents refuse to acknowledge the problem in an effort to protect their child. If the parents have negative views of dance, they usually excuse the child from accepting responsibility for inappropriate behavior.

- Because I am currently blessed with a principal who supports me, a final consequence for a child may be a visit to the principal. During this visit the student and the principal write a behavioral contract; then the student, principal, and parent or guardian all sign it. In this situation the behavior is documented. If the problem escalates, the principal calls the parents for a conference; the school counselor becomes involved; the child may have a one- to five-day in-house (in-school) suspension; and a three-day suspension from school could result depending on the severity of the problem.

- In the state of Washington there is a legislative bill called the Bauer Bill, which permits teachers to dismiss students who are out of control and disruptive in class. The responsibility for the child then falls on the administration. Investigate this concept in your state. If such a bill is not on the books, contact your state representative.

- When the majority of a class demonstrates an extreme lack of focus over an extended period of time and the students feed off of each other for inappropriate behavior, I resort to a written consequence method. As the students walk into the room they notice several desks with paper and pencils. Just the furniture produces appropriate behavior changes and shapes up the class. This method is known to produce fear of consequences—in some circles it is

frowned on, but in drastic situations one may need to take drastic measures.

1. The most effective writing assignment is encyclopedia work (*not* Internet work) during class or recess. In this assignment students who have consistently behaved inappropriately research some aspect of dance and write in their own words what they have read. I provide encyclopedias for a variety of reading levels. The students become engaged in the work; they do not disturb the class; and they stay involved until the project is completed (whenever that might be). They may even learn something.

2. Sometimes I require students to write an essay describing their behavior, appropriate behavior for dance class, and the steps they will take toward appropriate behavior. The length of the essay must be 30 to 50 words for third graders and increases with the grade level or ability. The paper must be neat, have complete sentences and proper punctuation, and communicate ideas about the topic. Usually, the principal must sign the essay before the student returns to class.

3. The challenge in using writing assignments as a consequence is that many students have trouble reading and writing,

and research assignments may be unsuitable consequences for them. On rare occasions when I have attempted all other possible solutions, I have not received support from the principal or the students' classroom teachers, and students have trouble reading, I have assigned to those students the old-fashioned method of writing lines: The students repeatedly write a sentence, such as, "I need to respect my classmates." This is one of the least desirable consequences. My intention for a consequence is for the assignment to be meaningful and somewhat related to dance.

 Tip

The punishment must fit the crime. Unless a student is violent toward himself or others, all inappropriate behaviors are actually minor offenses. Experiment with many different consequences until you find what works for your population. Before giving a consequence in anger, be aware that it usually mushrooms and can involve more students, teachers, the principal, and the parents. Even when you are angry, try to calmly give appropriate consequences. If you are not in total control of yourself, try asking the student to stand by the wall until you think of a consequence to fit her actions.

Trench Truth

On the first dance class of the year a second-grade boy who was new to the school bounded into the gym. Brian was very cute with his red hair, freckled face, and bulging green eyes. The students sat for the greeting. Brian decided that he would make a funny noise after each student's name was called. The students laughed the first few times. Once he realized that they were enjoying him, he made louder and weirder noises. I stopped and addressed him, letting him know that his noises were funny but inappropriate at this time. I continued with the names, and he continued the noises very quietly. Again, I stopped and told him that if he continued, he would be asked to stand by the wall away from the group. I called the next name, and he quietly whispered, "Eeek." Brian was immediately escorted to the wall. But it wasn't over yet, because he continued to make noises from the wall. I went close to him and again warned him of a more grave consequence such as a visit to the principal. I called the next name, and he repeated the name. I said, "Good-bye, Brian. You are going to see the principal." He made his body rigid and refused to move. After several minutes I walked to him and said, "I'm sorry, Brian, you have taken away too much time from the other students. You will need to go back to the classroom. I'm calling your teacher to let her know that you are on your way." As he was walking out of the room, he started yelling, "I'm going to see the principal. I'm not going to my teacher. And I'm never coming back to this dance class again. I don't want to do ballet and be in a dance recital." We could hear him yelling as he walked down the hall. It was the first and last time that I had to correct Brian that school year. He quickly learned the expectations for appropriate behavior and the consequences for inappropriate behavior.

Constructive Rest

There are many factors that can set students off task. Sometimes it appears that their energy is flying in a wild, uncontrolled manner. It could be that they are having a school assembly, the wind is blowing strongly, or they are having an off day.

 Obstacle

Surviving days when students are off task

 **Solutions**

- To center students and relax their energy, I begin my class with constructive rest, a technique in which one releases the body into gravity, helping to align the body and center its energy. The child lies on his back with the legs bent, knees coming together, and feet flat on the floor. The arms are folded across the chest or resting by the sides. I prefer to dim the lights and close out noise. This technique helps the students to relax and focus.

- When the giggling ceases and a sense of calm evolves, I begin a 2- to 5-minute relaxation exercise using imagery to help the students release tension and calm themselves. I begin by instructing them to feel the head resting on the floor; feel its weight and let it sink as if it were resting on a cloud. The exercise continues as I instruct students to release the jaw or the shoulders. The idea is to suggest tension release throughout the body. After the time allotted, I instruct the students to slowly move from the floor to a sitting position until they bring their focus back to the class.

- Some schools have mercury vapor lights that take 30 minutes to warm up to full power. Turning these lights off and on is inefficient. When this is the situation, I instruct the students to close their eyes and focus on the humming of the lights in their constructive rest positions.

 Tip

Introduce constructive rest when children are in first grade. Once they know the technique, you can rely on its benefits throughout their elementary school years. It is most helpful when you're not feeling well, there is a change in weather, the students arrive after a class party, or when tension or stress prevails in the room. Use this method; it worked for me.

Trench Truth

In public schools today there is little time when children are not required to be working. Constructive rest helps them relax and regroup themselves to deal with the next task. In first grade I introduce the technique to my afternoon classes. Many fall asleep during the constructive rest because they are so exhausted just trying to adapt to being in school for the whole day. I also like to use this technique when the barometric pressure changes. Children usually respond to the forces of nature, and constructive rest helps them to become more grounded. In fourth grade the students are involved in two weeks of state testing. The pressures on them to do their best are immense. Some have headaches, others go home sick, and some are so frightened that they cry. I use constructive rest at the beginning of their dance classes during those weeks. It helps relieve the stress and brings oxygen to their brains and "soul."

Teamwork

My goal in a class project is to make sure each student contributes to the creative process and then demonstrates or performs the project. When the project is completed, my goal is for each student to feel pride, not only about his or her own personal ideas and performance but also pride about the whole team. I call it the "team" because it represents a cooperative effort. I minimize the concept of starring roles at the elementary level; all my students are stars, because they work as a team. Learning to reach consensus, however, can be problematic for them.

 **Obstacle**

Getting past the boss

 **Solutions**

- I do not assign a leader of a group, but one or two people arise as leaders. Learning the difference between a leader and a boss is very difficult for children. Many children want to be the boss and to order everyone else in the group to perform their ideas. I emphasize to my students that leaders listen to the ideas of each group member and assist the group in organizing these ideas into a dance that will represent everyone in the group.

- Some students may create movements that other students either are not able to perform or may feel embarrassed about performing. I teach my students that they must consider the limitations and strengths of each person in the group. If the movement is to be done in unison, then it must be one that all of the students can perform. If the movement is not in unison, a variety of movements can be used. This movement can complement or frame the movements of another.

- In dance, the body is an instrument for expression. Being physically close to someone or touching someone's shoulder or hand may be difficult for some students. I understand that boys and girls giggle sometimes when they have to touch each other, but it helps their performance in dance class to get past the feelings that lead them to this behavior. Unfortunately, some children have been emotionally traumatized and are reluctant to touch others or be touched. It takes a long time to develop a trusting environment in a class. Children need to know that they can trust their teacher (and hopefully each other) and that they can feel safe in the class. I know I have established a trusting environment in my class when even the students who at first had problems begin to reach out to touch others and do not resist being touched.

Tip

Be involved in the interactions among your students when they are working in groups. If they appear to be on course, they can be on their own, but you need to periodically monitor each group.

Trench Truth

During my first teaching year in the Northwest, I divided the first graders into groups of three and instructed them to create shapes with hoops. There was a moment when all the students were engaged in the activity. I stepped back to observe the situation. Suddenly, three boys started to argue. Billy yelled at the other two students in his group. Johnny yanked the hoop away from the other two and turned his back. Then Sam pulled it away from Johnny and walked away trying to keep the other two from getting it. Sam dropped the hoop around his feet. He and Billy stood nose-to-nose, filled with anger; and they appeared to be in a face-off. Then Johnny entered their space and began slapping the other two on the head in a Three Stooges style. At that point I interceded. I immediately had the boys sit down (a method I use for getting their attention or for calming them). Two boys said that the third boy was bossing them around. I had them listen to and try the ideas of each boy. When they seemed to be communicating, I stepped away. During my first five years of teaching creative dance in this school, I constantly had to intervene in this way.

Steps to Cooperation and Collaboration

There are numerous methods of teaching cooperation and collaboration. The only successful methods include a steady, consistent approach.

 **Obstacle**

Finding methods to assure teamwork

Solutions

- The process of cooperation and collaboration begins in first grade. In my classes the students often work in pairs on assignments such as creating a project using two dance elements. I suggest that each student create a movement to go with one of the elements. For example, the elements may be ABAB, with *A* representing smooth, locomotor movement created by Allysia and *B* representing sharp, nonlocomotor movement created by Kylee. After each student has created the movement, they share their ideas and practice ABAB movements. As the group size increases, so do the required elements for the project. This method helps the students to understand the idea of sharing work and performing the ideas of others.

- Collaboration is the ultimate aim for group work. Each member expresses an idea and allows the group to experiment with it until it evolves into the whole group's idea. I usually demonstrate collaboration for the class. For example, I have two students join me in front of the class. We each suggest an idea, and then we perform them for the class. The class responds with suggestions. Then we ask questions such as, "What if you took the first movement and did it slowly or quickly?" We listen to and try the ideas of each group member and then revise the movement. The class views the movements and decides what looks best or what expresses the idea the best. This demonstration helps the students to understand the concept of collaboration.

- Many children cannot cope with losing their idea or having it changed until it is unrecognizable. But as time goes on they begin to realize that sometimes they can do their own movement and other times the group collaborates to change their movement. This collaborative process is quite long, and it is different from the way students function in their daily lives. But it is through this process that students express themselves, create new movements, and unite as a team. The goal of teamwork can be accomplished, and it has the power to change their lives!

 Tip

Collaboration spans many levels, and you need to teach it in small doses. The body, emotional maturity, the ego, leadership, the team, redesigned ideas, and movement trust are just some of the factors in developing cooperation and collaboration for dance and for life.

Trench Truth

I've had the joy of working with many students who understood collaboration. As we discussed ideas for a dance, I saw sparks of creative thoughts in their eyes. Without further instructions the students jumped up, gathered in groups of five or six students, and began working. I observed them discussing, pointing to the space, and then trying a variety of ideas. They had more discussion and then broke into smaller groups for a few minutes. They reconnected to share the parts of the dance and attempted to put them together.

One class created a dance called *From the Sublime to the Ridiculous.* The "sublime" dance started with a very slow procession of monks. The procession stopped and the monks leaned slowly from right to left until they all fell like dominoes. In the second ("ridiculous") part of the dance they came to life with small dances, such as the power of the shoes in which energy waves from the shoe paralyze the dancers; another group did a circus idea of pyramids, slides, and jumps; and another group did a tag dance. It was a delightful dance and was performed at the school district's dance gala.

Students who collaborate are heavenly. These students were happy and my job was to enjoy it. Please, send me more classes like those!

Logistics

In the early years of teaching in the Northwest, I allowed my students to casually enter the gym and join me in a circle. The behaviors that resulted were the running and sliding technique; the slow-walking, killing-time conversationalist method; the arguing act over the last place in line; and the avoidance routine, which included jumping from place to place rather than sitting next to a certain person. This style of entering the space and the lack of focus on dance grew longer as the weeks went on.

 **Obstacle**

Determining an effective method for entering the dance space

 **Solutions**

- I determine and set the space before the students enter the room. I ask myself these questions: Will the entire area be used for dance?

Where are the boundaries for movement? Will there be physical markings, cones, or painted lines that serve to mark the space? What will be the procedure for entering the space? How will the students find a working space?

- Over time I have developed a structured method for entering the dance space. I meet my students as they enter the space. I usually acknowledge them individually and instruct them to move quietly around the room. They walk single file (semi-military style) halfway around the gym on the painted line that sets the boundary for the dance space.

- When my students have entered the room, they face the wall and place their coats and other belongings on the floor. I usually say, "Place your coat in a small ball by the wall." Because of repeated lice epidemics, I instruct the students not to let their coats touch other coats. This eliminates their throwing the coats in a big pile. Although a big pile of clothing is all right in and of itself, I'm aiming for order, and the placement of the coats symbolizes the structure for the class.

- The students then proceed in their line around the room and file into a circle. The students stand in a circle because I have imposed an old Southern courtesy: Stand until the queen, the king, the president, the principal, or the teacher sits. We sit in a circle, but even sitting has a technique. The phrase is "Sitting requires two buns, right and left sides of the gluteus," or just "Two buns." (I have overheard first graders discussing dance, saying that they were required to sit on their biscuits.) Because we will sit for a short time, this method is comfortable enough. It discourages lying down, kneeling, sitting on their feet, and falling on others. These skills are a form of discipline and so is dance technique. The students begin to focus and center themselves the moment they enter the room, and they are ready to communicate and focus.

Tip

The sooner you decide on the logistics of entering the room, the more smoothly the class will progress. If you start off with a formal method, you can always ease up later.

 **Trench Truth**

I think of dance class as a preparation for other life situations. For example, I tell my students:

> In a few years, you'll be driving a car and I'll be a little old lady. If I'm trying to get on the highway, I hope you'll let me merge into the lane of traffic. So beginning today, we will learn to merge."

As they proceed around the circle I say, "Each car needs to let another merge into the circle of traffic." Sometimes I pretend to be the merging ramp traffic light. I drop the red light (my arm) in front of them and lift it when it is their turn to merge. They need to be alert and ready to merge, or they will miss their turn. This method separates seemingly inseparable friends and teaches the students to be polite when they actually begin to drive a car one day. I call out phrases that keep them alert to driving: "Please stay on the road (painted line)." "Don't drive on the shoulder of the road." "Put down the cell phone and focus on driving." When all are on the circle, we stop and assure each car of a parking space. Each needs to be able to open the car doors 6 inches. Each car cannot bump or scratch the one next to it, nor can it "hog" the parking spaces. This is a game that I hope will slip into their subconscious and will help develop awareness of the skills needed for driving.

Creating a Dance Space

Preparing the Space

The physical environment sets the tone of the dance program. Many dance educators teach in a cafeteria, gym, or classroom. The task is to convert the multipurpose environment into a dance space.

 **Obstacle**

Getting the space ready for dance class

 **Solutions**

- In most cases, the basic approach is to create a mental change within the students. I attempt to create a dance attitude by always referring to the students as "the dancers." The term is considered an honor and the students respond accordingly. The room is always called "the dance space" whether it is the gym, cafeteria, or classroom.

- Every day I set up the facility for safety. This includes dust mopping or wet mopping areas of the room (if the maintenance person didn't have time) and moving furniture that may be in the way or may be a distraction for the students.

- Before I begin my classes, I organize the room with the equipment needed for the period or for the entire morning or afternoon when there is no break time. I have a rolling cart on which I place a boom box or compact disc player, tapes and compact discs, chalk and erasers, pencils and paper, lesson plans, and felt-tip markers. Also ready to roll is a two-sided board: on one side is a green slate board or a dry-erase board, and on the other side is a bulletin board on which I hang photos and charts. I also set up a microphone, drums, props, a video camera, a videocassette recorder, and a monitor. When the room and equipment are organized, it is easier to focus on the students and on teaching the lesson. I can supervise the students during the entire class, because I rarely leave the room for supplies.

- I decorate the room with dance photos and terminology. Using laminated charts and photos that can be placed securely on the walls increases their lifetime. I also place some charts on the inside of a closet door that can be opened for use and locked away when I'm not in that building.

- Efficiency is most important in setting up, especially if you need to move from one space or one school to another. I use carts or chalkboards with wheels for easy maneuvering. Find a method to set up vocabulary quickly. I have used lightweight sentence strip holders that roll up and have clear plastic strips that support word cards. These strip holders can be purchased at teacher supply stores.

 Tip

Consult with the principal and the maintenance person regarding the safety of using gym walls for charts. When community groups use the dance facility, charts and pictures tend to vanish.

 **Trench Truth**

It is often difficult to share space with other teachers. When community groups are involved, the situation can worsen. We often have community groups using the gym at night and on weekends. The physical education teacher and I noticed that on several Wednesday mornings things were moved about in our office (which is a storeroom). We told the night maintenance man, who said that the scouts use the gym on Tuesday nights. Thinking that it could be one of the scouts, he decided to catch the person in action. He hid in our office behind a rack of balls while the scouts were having their meeting. Soon, he heard the scout leader telling a child, "I use my credit card to unlock the door." The door opened and in came the scout leader and three kids, who helped themselves to balls. The maintenance man started to laugh at the ridiculousness of such a leader. The leader didn't even notice him there; they took the equipment and left. With this eyewitness account, the leader was fired and we got heavy-duty locks on our door.

Sharing the Space

When a facility is used for many different teaching experiences, it is difficult to adapt it for dance classes. An initial problem for me was that the gym was used for both physical education and dance classes. In many schools the classroom teacher taught physical education. A classroom teacher or the maintenance person taught the intramural program after school. The games that were played followed the standard rules, but the classes were relaxed and loosely organized. The students were free to drink, go to the bathroom, and scream or yell when they desired. Then I arrived and my dance class intruded on the space with its order and more controlled requirements. Thus began an ongoing struggle between a relaxed setting and a structured dance class.

 **Obstacle**

Struggling for the territory

 **Solutions**

- For many dance and physical education teachers, sharing the gym and cafeteria becomes a territorial struggle. But in the schools that had physical education teachers, we were able to solve the problem by considering the sizes of the children. To assure free and safe movement, third through fifth grades had priority to the gym for both dance and physical education. In determining the gym schedule, we had to consider the time needed for setting up equipment at various grade levels. We had to be flexible; a lot of give and take is necessary for the space and schedules to work for both dance and physical education.
- If the space is used for physical education, creative dance, and other activities, I try to negotiate with the other teachers on the rules and procedures for the space. The physical education teacher and I have agreed on certain procedures that are enforced in the gym and cafeteria spaces: When they enter the space their coats are folded and placed in a personal space by the wall. No one is allowed to leave the room without permission. Students quietly enter and leave in a line. All students must wear clothing appropriate for dance. They are not allowed to slide on their knees across

the room. They are not allowed to crash into the walls. Because these procedures are established and enforced by the two of us, behavior is consistent. The students are not engaged in manipulative behaviors, such as saying, "The physical education teacher lets us do such and such."

 Tip

Communicate with everyone who uses the space about procedures. Remember, there must be give and take on all sides for the situation to work.

 **Trench Truth**

Recently I went to a basketball game with a friend. Not being an avid sports spectator, I was unaware of the agenda of professional sport. An astonishing occurrence was that every time the teams ran to the other side of the court, two or three young people ran out with dust mops or towels and wiped the floor. After inquiring about this peculiar ritual, my friend told me that the floor had to be free from sweat to prevent

slipping. I perceived this as an odd thought. In a dance performance, the floor is full of sweat and no one wipes it up. Sweat is dripping from the dancers' bodies as they make contact by lifting, swinging, and throwing each other. But dance artists are underpaid and their sweat is unacknowledged. I suppose that when millions of dollars are spent on professional sports, sweat receives great acknowledgment.

As the game progressed, it was obvious to me that I live on an unconventional plane. Every time the visiting team was to shoot the ball, the music disc jockey played music from "Jaws" while the commentator harassed the players. The aggression grew as the game intensified. I have experienced cheerleading with the crowds yelling, cheering, booing and hissing; but this behavior of the home team officials blew me away.

My professional energies are in teaching respect, encouragement, acceptance, positive critique, and good sporting behavior; and this experience jolted me into the reality of why my job is so difficult. Professional sports pay high salaries for people to antagonize each other—it's part of the game, they tell me.

Establishing Boundaries

Boundaries give structure to a class. Without boundaries, the students crash into the wall, leave the room, run across the stage, and climb on all objects in sight. For kindergarteners and first-grade students, entering a gym for the first time is like setting them free in a candy store. Their eyes enlarge, and for many children there is a sudden rush of sheer delight. It is not unusual to see extreme responses, from running uncontrollably to freezing in terror.

 **Obstacle**

Establishing a safe environment

 **Solutions**

- I establish a secure environment for the little ones by limiting their space. Using the orange cones from the safety patrol department, I divide the space into a smaller section. I place the cones on a line that is painted on the gym floor.

- I introduce the dance space to the students through the relationship of the orange safety cones seen on the roads and how they symbolize danger:

    If your mom is driving her car along the road and sees orange cones, she usually slows down and does not drive through the cones. If she drove past the cones, the car could fall into a big hole, so she needs to be aware of the cones because they tell her that danger is close by. The cones have the same meaning for dance class. You may not cross the cones or you will be in danger.

- One child always asks what the danger is or what will happen if he crosses the cones. My response is that the student who crosses the cones will miss the class. Usually one or two students will test this response to see exactly what this means. If students intentionally go out of the boundaries, I immediately take them out of the dance. They quickly learn that I follow through on the rules and consequences. If students move outside the cones because they appear to be unaware of the space, I pause to give the class a gentle reminder of the boundaries.

- When the students are aware of the space and the class understands the boundaries, I remove the cones. The painted lines or the centerline on the gym floor then mark the boundaries. For older students, I only use the cones to establish performance space. The size of the space changes according to the dance or topic of the class.

- I change the boundaries frequently to encourage the students to be aware of the space.

 Tip

Once you have established the boundaries, enforce them. You will help your students develop spatial awareness.

 Trench Truth

When teaching I refer to boundaries as the ends of the stage:

> If you dance past the boundary, you will fall into a hole at the end of the stage that is the orchestra pit. "What is the orchestra pit?" you may ask. Well, the orchestra pit is a hole at the end of the stage that is about 5 or 6 feet deep. The orchestra sits in the pit to play the music for dance or for plays. When you dance on a stage, you will need to be very careful not to go too close to the end of the stage. If you fall into the pit, you'll probably break your leg.

Another boundary I emphasize is the side of the stage. I may say:

> If you dance to the very end of the dance space, you will be dancing in the wings, which means that you'll be behind the curtain and your mom and dad will not see you.

I put the concept of space in context with dance, so the students will be prepared if they ever dance on a stage.

Creating Personal Space

The use of space is very important in a dance class setting; how you establish the space will set the tone for the class. Children do not understand the concept of moving apart or spreading out. They think that if another child is 3 inches away, they have plenty of space. This is truly fine until they start bumping into each other by accident or intentionally.

 **Obstacle**

Finding a personal space

 **Solutions**

- Sally Mundinger, a physical education teacher in West Bend, Wisconsin, shared the following organizational secret with me, and I have used it for many years: At the beginning of each school year, I create a personal space for each student using white liquid shoe polish to draw dots or geometric shapes on the floor. I mark each row and each line of dots about 8 or 9 feet apart. I stagger the rows so I can easily view the students

```
   o    o    o    o
      o    o    o
   o    o    o    o
      o    o    o
```

It initially takes about 30 minutes to set up. I use these dots throughout the school year and touch them up periodically. The dots take about 30 minutes to dry. I have one dot or design for each student. The students are allowed to choose a mark each time they enter the dance space. Doing this establishes freedom of choice, a personal space, and a place that ensures safety and order.

- Another benefit is that the shoe polish can be cleaned with floor cleanser or comes off easily when the floors are stripped for waxing. This makes the maintenance crew happy.

Tip

Allow the students to choose their own spaces. If they demonstrate that they are unable to make *wise choices* for placement, then assigned places may be necessary.

Trench Truth

When I arrived to teach in a high-risk school, I noticed that students had no sense of personal space. They were always a breath away from another. This situation allowed for poking, pushing, hitting, blowing, bumping, and other disrespectful behaviors. I sat down with each class and discussed the situation. I told them that I had worked in many schools in the city but had never seen children poking each other constantly. We discussed the necessity of space, the way you feel when someone is in your space, and reasons they needed to be so close. I think that most were amazed that someone would discuss it with them. We developed a motto that was chanted throughout the year: "No more poking is our motto." I didn't think it would affect them, but it caught on and the poking was reduced dramatically.

Dancing in Mashed Potatoes

Most dancers are plagued with the problem of finding space to dance. The dance educator in the public schools is no exception. Although a gym or cafeteria may be provided, these spaces bring their own inconveniences. I have conducted classes on grass, in hallways, on small stages, and in music rooms. Some spaces are a safety hazard, such as small or portable classrooms filled with desks, damp covered outdoor areas, and blacktop playgrounds. Adapting to the provided dance space assists students in developing the flexibility that is needed in performances, but it also provides another obstacle for the dance educator to overcome. Flying through the air from hardwood sprung floors is usually not the situation in elementary schools. Many gyms are furnished with tiled floors or a rubberized floor covering laid over concrete. The large space of the gym is the most rewarding feature, but jumping on concrete for any length of time takes its toll on the body and drains everyone's energy level. Noise is another joy of the gym. I think that architects design these structures to enhance the full sound of cheering, which encourages athletes. Smells! Noises! Tendinitis! Oh, and traffic, I forgot to mention the traffic. In some schools, classrooms are attached to the gym or cafeteria. In this physical construction, the gym becomes a major thoroughfare for school traffic. Students walk escorted or run unescorted through the gym to their classes. Adults also seem to enjoy observing how cute the children are when dancing, and they find reasons to slowly meander through the space. Appreciation of dance is one of the goals of the program, but keeping the dancers on task with so many outside distractions is a challenge.

 **Obstacle**

Adapting to the space

 **Solutions**

- The hardness of the gym floor tends to inhibit the students' movement. Other than sliding across the room on their knees and crashing against the walls, students are concerned that they may become injured while dancing. They, therefore, tend to take fewer risks in floor work and partner contact work, unless I provide them with tumbling mats. I also continuously encourage my students to wear clothing and shoes that will provide safety in the space.

- The texture of the floor is a feature that tends to change throughout the day. Elementary students enjoy a mid-morning or afternoon recess that outfits them in sand, wet grass, dirt, rocks, and wood chips. As they enter the gym for dance class, remnants of their jubilant experiences fall from their bodies. A large dust mop is always available and I frequently trail after them with it in order for the class to proceed in a somewhat clean space.

 Tip

If administrators have never been involved with dance, they probably don't understand the spatial needs. Don't give up the quest for adequate facilities. Educate teachers and administrators with specific examples.

Trench Truth

I have been unfortunate enough to teach in a gym that in some cases has doubled as a cafeteria. The environment offers challenging episodes that activate the senses with the clanging of pots and tantalizing aromas. As the morning begins, croutons with garlic are toasted and cinnamon buns are baked in the oven, stimulating the salivary glands. While class is in session the maintenance person begins to set up for lunch, rolling wheeled tables and benches across the dance floor. The space shrinks, and the dancers are surrounded by the reality of a cafeteria. As the class is winding down, an audience arrives. The first lunch group will have free entertainment while they munch. The teaching time is over, and the performance or student shutdown instantly follows.

The afternoon classes commence in an environment created by the smells of lunch garbage and the sounds of dishes being sprayed and clinking through the dishwasher. The maintenance person usually has 10 minutes in which to clean the cafeteria after lunch. Due to this rushed procedure, the space offers a variety of textures to the pitter-patter of little feet. Gelatin squares bounce across the floor. Spaghetti curls like worms. Banana chunks provide a sliding feature. Spilled Slurpee® glues feet to the floor, and mashed potatoes become more than a dance from the 1960s. The whipped peaks of potatoes are hardened by grains of sand and create little mountain ranges that remain plastered to the floor. Classes begin by dodging the residue and tiptoeing through mopped wetness.

I've had nightmares where I am wading through garbage while teaching. As my worn-out sweat clothes attempted to camouflage the food deposits, I found myself knee deep in mashed potatoes as an avalanche of green peas rushed down on me. The peas became soccer balls, but I was unable to kick them because the Slurpee held my feet firmly in place.

Other Spatial Concerns

The environment of the room has an effect on the energy the students exert, and consequently on the way they dance. Light, sound, and temperature affect the quality of the class. For example, if the room is dark or dreary, the students' energy tends to be low; if it is very noisy, their energy tends to be chaotic. As the temperature rises and cools, students' energy works in reverse: hot equals low energy and cool equals high energy.

 **Obstacle**

Adapting the environment for the class

 **Solutions**

- I set up the room to create an upbeat, energy-filled mood. I turn on every light in the gym; I open curtains that usually cover windows; and if weather permits, I open the doors. The darker the room, the more difficult it is for me to be energetic.

- In a creative dance program where students are involved in collaborative activities, the noise level appears to grow. After weeks or months of teaching them to work together, I see an amazing change occur: All students become engaged in the project—there is focused conversation, not yelling at each other—and the volume level is appropriate.

- Determining a working volume is not an overnight procedure. Many factors affect volume, such as cooperative decision making, time allowance, acoustics, and the number of students in a small group. In one school, I noticed that the children were exceptionally loud and appeared to be yelling when working in small groups. The noise level remained constant no matter which class was in the gym. After observation, I realized that there was an acoustical problem that magnified a whisper to a scream. One solution for this problem is to use acoustical foam or carpet squares on the walls to reduce the noise level.

- Some children, such as special education students, are sometimes unable to work in large, bright spaces. They are distracted or unable to control themselves. I attempt to make adjustments for these students by reducing the space with the safety cones. I also adjust the light and keep out noises whenever possible.

- I have found that working with groups of a few special education students in a smaller space has produced the best results.
- I place my hand on a child's shoulders or back to keep her in touch with her personal body space. I stand close to particular children with learning problems while giving instructions. I may ask a question of a particular child and give him time to process the information. I say, "Think about this, and I'll be back for the answer." I return about 15 to 20 seconds later to hear his thoughts. I try to listen to the comments and concerns of children with problems by allowing them time to voice them.

 Tip

Dance is a kinesthetic art form. Special issues regarding touching, holding, and being close always arise. Address these concerns with the principal.

 Trench Truth

Teachers need to be careful when touching students. Recently, the news media has been filled with cases of sexual and physical child abuse. I have known some teachers who were accused of improper touching. Some students accuse because they don't like the teacher, because it gets them attention, or because it makes good conversation. Whatever their reasons are, it does happen, and it can bring devastating results.

The following story is probably the most upsetting experience of my teaching career. It brought me to tears and made me shake with fear. I wondered whether I would lose my job.

It was the most disconcerting class of the morning. The fourth-grade students were to complete assignments from the previous week. Many were arguing in their groups, others were refusing to work, and one was so upset with her group that she was throwing a tantrum. It seemed that all the fires were put out when the students began to show their work.

A group of students took their dance places. A boy who was sitting on his feet about 12 inches in front of me was engaged in loud conversation. I called his name three times, but he appeared not to hear me. So I stretched my leg and tapped him on his foot with my foot. I tapped twice to get his attention. He looked up to acknowledge me and turned away rather nonchalantly. The students showed their work, and all left for recess.

About 10 minutes later the principal stormed into the gym. He delivered the news that the boy said that I had kicked him in the back, and his friends who were eyewitnesses agreed. My instruction from the principal was to call the boy's parents and explain what had happened before the child got home.

I explained the situation to the boy's mother, and she said that it didn't sound right to her, because her child would never lie. By lunchtime the boy's parents were in the principal's office. I entered, acknowledged the parents, and sat quietly. The boy entered the room and started to cry. The father handled the situation by asking the boy to explain what had happened. The boy retold his story, which resembled what had actually happened. The father asked, "How hard did the teacher kick you—was it like a football kick, or was it a tap?" The boy said it was a tap. Then the father asked, "Did the teacher hurt you or hurt your feelings?" The child said that I had hurt his feelings. At that moment, the tension was released from my shoulders and I began to breathe again. The father then talked to the boy about how stories grow and get out of hand. The boy sobbed. It appeared that it was easier for him to look important to his friends than to tell the truth.

The father was excellent in his problem-solving approach, and the mother was able to understand that her child was not totally honest and was caught up in the emotion of the moment. The problem was solved. The boy and I were able to have a much stronger working relationship. However, it was the first time I realized that a class of fourth graders could hang me. It was their word against mine. Subsequently, I began to have less and less physical contact with my students.

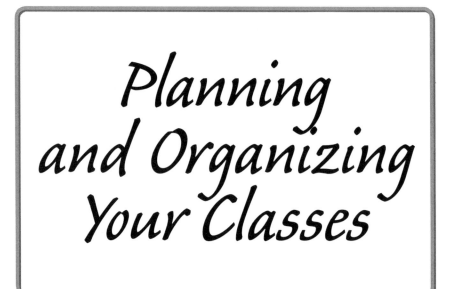

Planning and Organizing Your Classes

Where Do I Start?

Each school and every class within the school is different. The students will have different challenges at the beginning of the year. Usually, a struggle arises for class roles as the leader, the clown, the smartest, or the most troublesome. Many students act silly because they are working with new children, and others want to spend time seeing old friends. Many are ready to dance.

 **Obstacle**

Beginning each school year

 **Solutions**

- With a transient population and new class groupings, the need to review everything from rules to concepts was essential. All new students brought with them both positive and negative behaviors from their summers and from their previous schools. Working the new students into a dance program took time, but they should progressed quickly because the other students knew my expectations.

- At the beginning of each school year, I assume that the students know little about dance. I take time to move through elements and concepts while focusing on uniting the class as a team. I keep the classes upbeat and fast moving while directing their attention to the use of space and respect for others. Depending on the grade level, it takes a few weeks to review the elements and concepts of dance and to get all students on board for the year.

- As the students dance, I gently remind them of self-management rules (see chapter 2). When problems arise, I may stop the class and discuss what happened, or I may address it at the beginning of the next class as part of class procedures or rules. It all depends on the severity of the concern.

- When I put great emphasis on establishing the class environment through learning the rules and procedures and reviewing the dance elements and concepts during the first few weeks, the rest of the year was filled with rich dance experiences.

Tip

The first six weeks of the school year are exhausting because it takes total focus, dedication, and commitment to each minute. Take care of yourself during this time.

Trench Truth

When I started the dance program, kindergarteners through third graders appeared open to the experience of creative dance. The fourth and fifth graders, however, were quite a different story. Many students entered the class with great apprehension about this new experience. Many hid their fears with rowdy, silly, or resistant behavior. Their views of dance were set and were quite negative. It was a struggle to get them to cooperate. They soaked up an extreme amount of my energy as I was continually coaxing, prodding, encouraging, and disciplining. Providing these students with activities that gave them positive dance experiences and fostered a gentle change of view required much patience.

Throughout my lesson plans, I wrote myself notes: "Get control of them." "Too wild." "So silly." When they moved across the room,

many would race, crash into other students, or scream as they moved. Everything was a race to see who were the fastest, the loudest, and the silliest. The students' focus on most activities was short-lived. Eager eyes and silly looks shot around the room as they responded by laughing at each other and taking cues such as when to bump, smash, and trip each other.

After two months, my interpretation was that the students were afraid of the demands of this new curriculum, were self-conscious about moving and creating in front of their peers, and lacked awareness of the possibilities dance offered.

Who Are These Kids, Anyway?

In my early years of teaching in two schools, it was difficult to remember the names of all 900 students. Teaching in two schools made it more confusing. Until I knew the students, they were a mass of people who all looked alike. I left one school and went to the other, and it appeared that I had seen some of the same students at the first school. I make a valiant attempt to know each student.

 **Obstacle**

Knowing the students' names

 **Solutions**

- When the students enter the dance class we sit in a circle, and I attempt to acknowledge each student by name. Knowing the students' names is essential because as the students move through the space they will need to be acknowledged. It is difficult to get attention by yelling out, "Hey, girl in the red T-shirt, good job."

- My method for remembering names is to ask a few students to say their names and then test myself. I add a couple of new names to my memory during each class. Once I have committed a few names to memory, I ask each child for the first letter of his name. This helps me to place the name in a smaller category. Then, in two or three guesses I get it right. The odder the name, the easier it is for me to remember. By putting forth an extreme amount of effort, it took four months to become able to remember each student's name during the first year. I usually say the names at every class to refresh my memory, to acknowledge the new students, and to personalize the class. This activity originally took about 8 minutes, but now I am able to acknowledge each student on sight in 2 minutes. After I acknowledge each student by name, I address the announcements, the concerns of the class, and the topic of the day. By this time (4 to 5 very valuable minutes into the class) the students are focused and calm, and they know the expectations.

- When I arrive in a new school or when I have students whose names I have difficulty remembering, I ask them to tell me their names whenever they see me in the building. If a child takes the

- John, Jason, Jeff...

time to personalize herself, I usually remember who she is by the next class.

- Another method of remembering the names is to get the class pictures that are taken at the beginning of the year and have the students' names listed with them. Then I review the names in my spare time or before the class walks into the room.

Tip

The students know that you care when you know their names. It also helps when a parent calls and you actually know his child's name.

Trench Truth

To complicate the matter of remembering names, in each grade level the students' first names were taken from movies and soap operas that were popular the year they were born. Several students had the same name or a variation of the name, such as Kaylee, Kaylyn, Katie, Kayla; Alexis, Alexia, Alexa, Alliegha, Alex; or Jacob, Josh, Jordan, Justin, Jason.

Class Procedures

As my students work on movement progressions across the room, I teach and enforce dance etiquette. The etiquette includes all the procedures that are expected in order for the class to move along smoothly with respect to all students.

 **Obstacle**

Using line manners

 **Solutions**

- I usually introduce line manners to my students early in first grade, and every time the situation arises thereafter I tell them the following:

  If you go to a dance class anywhere in the world, the line rules will be the same: The dancers stand in three, four, or five lines. One person from each line moves across the floor at the same time. When they get to the other side of the room they either stop and form a new line, or they walk around the outside of the dance space and go to the end of their line.

  While waiting for their turn to dance, the dancers stand and watch the other dancers. In dance you either do dance or watch dance. You can learn a lot about a movement by observing others performing it.

  When dancers have respect for each other, they don't stick their feet out to trip the other dancers as they come down the aisle; and they don't high-five or poke the other dancers as they pass by. High fives are great in sports, but they are usually not part of a creative dance class.

  When the dancers have finished the movement across the room, they stop before they get to the other dancers, and they walk down the aisle to the end of the line. No one slides down the aisle to his place. And no one runs and crashes against the wall or the sports mats.

- After I have introduced the line rules, I reiterate them by acting them out in a humorous manner. I reinforce them by complimenting the students as they progress to their places in line, or I may stop the class to remind them of the rules as some child goes sliding down the aisle.

 Tip

Be clear about how your students are to line up and where they are to go after they move across the room.

 Trench Truth

Many aspects of sports are similar to those of dance; however, establishing the discipline of dance is different from what I have noticed in sports. Maybe I just don't understand the logic behind sports etiquette. For example, I still haven't figured out why there are mats on the gym walls. If students were taught to be aware of their space, they wouldn't need to crash against the wall.

Also, as I mention in my introduction to line manners, giving high fives, which is often done in sports, is usually not part of a creative dance class. This behavior is found in some forms of dance and in some cultures. However, in an elementary school setting, once the students start giving high fives, the act of giving high fives becomes the goal rather than the dance itself. I have also found that it becomes a competitive gesture that discourages those who do not earn high fives from their peers. Giving high fives develops an aggressive, competitive nature rather than the expressive, collaborative nature that I try to foster. I usually discourage giving high fives in the early grades, and as the students get older I gradually let it slip in, depending on the dance movement that we are doing. For example, if we are doing African dance or hip-hop where a competitive feeling is generated, the students naturally give high fives to compliment one another.

Clothing

The best way to ensure clothing will be appropriate for safe movement in the dance space is to consult with school district authorities about the legalities of dress codes. Using this approach will help you gain the support of your administration when you decide what to ask your students to wear to dance class.

 **Obstacle**

Getting the students to wear appropriate and safe clothing for dance

 **Solutions**

- Depending on the floor and the safety of the situation, I may ask my students to be barefoot. But dancing barefoot can bring other health problems depending on the students' level of cleanliness. Some children have warts, athlete's foot, or other contagious diseases. I require my students to wear a tennis shoe style: lightweight, rubber-soled shoes that use laces or Velcro® closures. Shoes that do not give support to the foot will be unsafe, and if a student sprains an ankle or twists a knee, I am ultimately responsible for the injury.

- An excellent choice for dance clothing is commercial dancewear. But in most public school situations there is no time to change clothing. Shirts and sweat pants or pants that provide freedom of movement may be all that I can require. If girls are wearing skirts or dresses, I require them to wear shorts under them for freedom of movement. If I don't enforce this requirement, they will find excuses for not moving, they will move less freely out of modesty, or they will cry that someone is looking up their skirts.

- Safety concerns in regard to clothing change with the styles. Currently, the style for young people is to have pants drag on the ground. This type of clothing is a safety hazard and is not permitted in my dance class. To avoid tripping, my students must cuff their pants or hem them with safety pins if the pants touch the ground. Some of my students like to wear a parent's shirt with the sleeves hanging 12 inches below the hands. I require that all shirtsleeves be rolled up for safety.

- Once I have established the dress code, I know I must enforce it. If I continuously accept excuses, my students will know that this procedure does not really apply. I usually remind the younger students about appropriate dance clothing throughout their first-grade year. Eight months later, the reminding period is over and they will have to accept the same consequence as older students—to sit out of the dance class. Usually a child needs to sit out only once before beginning to remember to wear appropriate clothing. Once I have enforced the dress code, my students keep each other in check.

 Tip

Because I teach so many classes, it is easy to forget what I told each class. So I ask the class to remind me the next week that I said, "Whoever does not wear their tennis shoes will sit by the wall." Once you have established the dress code and the consequence for not following it, let the students assist you in enforcing it.

Trench Truth

For three years I taught Lynette, who always tested boundaries with clothing. She came to dance class in platform shoes, sandals, slip-ons, or high heels. Occasionally, she wore tennis shoes and was able to participate. At the end of the second year, Lynette came to class with sandal-style tennis shoes. She waited for my response to her breaking the dress code. I was caught off guard, and I said, "Oh, I've never seen tennis shoes like those." Then I continued with the class.

The following year, Lynette's parents came in for a conference, because they said that I embarrassed her when I corrected one of her movements. During the conference, her mother said that I was always picking on her child about something, especially her shoes. Then came the clincher: "Last year, I told Lynette that we were going to get her the sandal-style tennis shoes just to see what you would say. And you said, 'Oh, I've never seen tennis shoes like those.'" I realized then that Lynette's mother had sacrificed her daughter's education to make a point about the shoes and to reinforce an attitude of disregard for rules and requirements. This type of parental guidance happens often. Parents are teaching children that rules do not apply to them and no one can make them comply. Unfortunately, the children are the victims because they are caught between expectations of school authorities and the parent.

I have confronted these situations with kindness, logic, and school rules, but it has usually been to no avail. I have found the best results when the principal deals with this type of situation.

Methods for Grouping

One of the most useful but difficult aspects of creative dance is learning to work cooperatively. In the regular classroom, group or partner work is usually set up so that a more advanced student assists a student who needs help. Another classroom method is pairing friends or students of like minds. I have noticed that classroom teachers avoid pairing students together who don't get along with each other. In my dance classes, I have an entirely different view of grouping and partnering. I believe that working with a variety of people is an opportunity for growth, and I like to give my students as many different growing opportunities as possible. Students usually run to their best friend when they hear the announcement that they should have a partner. I occasionally allow students to work with their friends, but my goal is for the students to work with a variety of people. There are many methods for quickly grouping students.

 **Obstacle**

Pairing partners

 **Solutions**

- Before my students look for a partner or group, I instruct them to sit back-to-back when they find a partner. Because they are partnered sitting down, it becomes obvious to me who is still looking for a partner.

- I instruct my students to find partners based on various factors. Here are some examples: "Find a partner who is the same size as you are; who is the opposite size of you; who is wearing the same color shirt as you are; who has the same color eyes as you do; who is the person of your choice."

- I instruct my students to form two lines parallel to each other, and I say, "The person next to you is your partner," or "The person behind you in line is your partner."

- I assign each member of one half of the class a number (for example, from 1 to 12); I also assign the other half the numbers 1 to 12. The students with like numbers are partners.

- I instruct my students to group themselves by telling them, "You have 5 beats to create a group that has two boys and two girls," or "You have 5 beats to create a group of two tall students and one short student."

- I instruct my students to count off to five or six, depending on the number of students who will be in each group. After the count, the ones form a group, then the twos, then the threes, and so on. When I use this method, the grouping is random.

- To separate disruptive students from each other, I place each disruptive student at the head of a line. The other students are assigned to form lines of four people behind the line leaders, or they may be assigned to stand in a certain line. Each line becomes a group. The disruptive students are separated, and they tend to assume some responsibility because they are line leaders.

 Tip

Use a variety of grouping techniques. However, to reduce stress, do allow the students to occasionally choose their best friends.

 **Trench Truth**

I once had a student named Heather, a very awkward girl who had many difficulties. Most of the children did not want to work with her. I made Heather one of five line leaders. Each line needed five students. On this particular day I called each student by name and each one chose a line leader. I called six students and Heather had no one in her line. Then I called eight-year-old Zak, who was one of the most popular boys in the class. Zak chose Heather's line. In a short time Heather's line was filled. The students performed the activity, and when the class was over I asked Zak why he had chosen to be in Heather's line. Zak said, "I chose her because I didn't want her to feel hurt. I also knew that other boys would come to be on the team if I was there." Many young children have true compassion.

Charts

Using charts was one of my best methods for keeping my students aware of dance elements and concepts. The charts are based on the guidelines established in National Dance Standards.

 **Obstacle**

Using charts

 **Solutions**

- I label five large pieces of colored paper (2 1/2 feet by 4 feet) Space, Energy, Time, Form, and Concepts. Charts 5.1 through 5.5 suggest some of the vocabulary that I use with my students. I have them laminated to prevent tearing, and I attach them to a wall with masking tape. In some schools I've had to put these up daily, because the night community groups would tear them off the wall. As the students are introduced to different elements and concepts, I write or draw pictures on the appropriate charts. The students use the charts as a reference in the creative process.
- Jän Abramavitz, a creative dance educator in Vancouver, Washington, shared with me the idea for a choreographic tips chart (see chart 5.6). The students are able to refer to this chart to get ideas for expanding their movement phrases or to get a different perspective of the same movement.

 Tip

Begin using the charts as you introduce the elements and concepts.

 **Trench Truth**

When the students are involved in setting the rubrics for a dance, we examine the charts and choose several elements that we want to demonstrate, or we may base the dance on a general concept. If the students are creating their own work, they are free to choose from the charts.

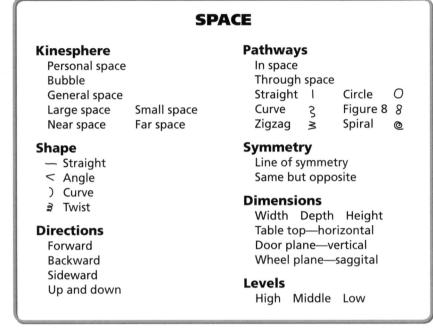

Chart 5.1

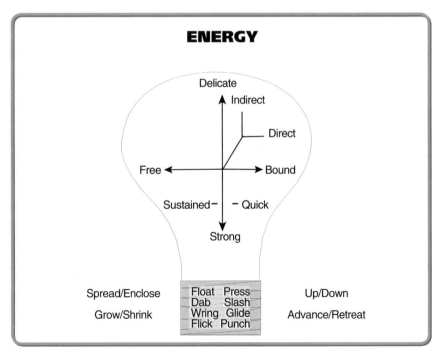

Chart 5.2

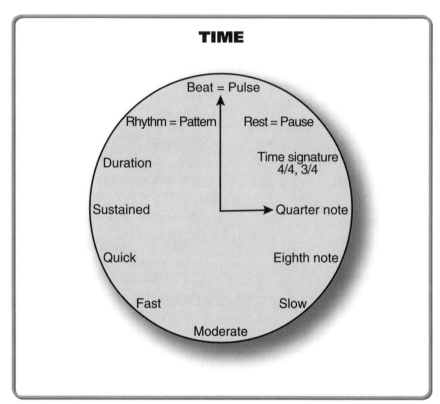

Chart 5.3

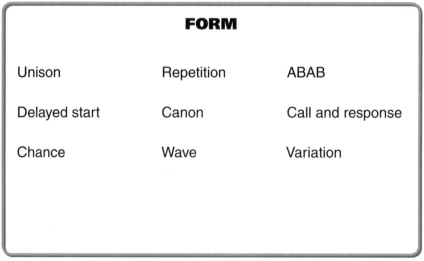

Chart 5.4

CONCEPTS

Balance (resist gravity)
Weight
Muscles
Shift weight
Base of support
Mass: has weight and occupies
    space

Weight share
Toss
Avoid
Embrace
Shape
Travel

Counterbalance (one weight supporting another)
Push/pull
Equal weight
Equal force
Pressure

Contrasts
Fast/slow
Over/under
Expand/shrink
Together/apart

Chart 5.5

TIPS FOR CHOREOGRAPHY

- Make the movement . . .
    bigger.
    smaller.
    faster.
    slower.
- Change the . . .
    level.
    facing.
    pathway.
    direction.
    body part.
    rhythm.

- Turn the movement.
- Use gestures.
- Repeat the . . .
    phrase.
    part of the phrase.
- Reverse the . . .
    phrase.
    part of the phrase.

Chart 5.6

Lesson Plans

A lesson plan should be a workable, flexible plan that shows where the class has been and where it is going. Objectives and goals and how these relate help you establish guidelines, and related activities determine the path.

 **Obstacle**

Organizing lesson plans

 **Solutions**

- The first year that I taught creative dance in the schools, I was given the same style lesson plan book that was used by the classroom teachers. The book had 15 boxes on each page, and I was to write the plan for each class in a separate box. I was teaching 30 classes per week. I tried to write general lesson plans for each grade level, but I felt confined in the little boxes and desperately needed writing space. By the fourth week of school, I was using a page for each grade level and disregarded the little squares. At this rate, I foresaw that I would need several lesson plan books for the year.

  The following year I invested in a three-ring binder with pocket dividers for each class. Each section began with a class list, followed by general concepts that were introduced to the students during the previous years. At a glance, I knew where the students had been and was able to build on these concepts during the year. I use loose-leaf paper to write each lesson plan. The plan is a general statement about the elements and concepts to be explored and the activities that may be used to introduce and reinforce them. If I use the same plan for all classes at a particular grade level, I simply make copies and insert them where needed.

  By organizing my lesson plans in a binder, I am able to write about the creative process of each class. It also helps to have the plans for all classes in the same book, because I can track students' progress and stay on course with my plan. When working with ongoing projects for primary grades, I jot down the names of students and their partners or groups, because many young children cannot remember whom they worked with the previous week. I also draw pictures or dance maps, take notes about class management, and record strengths and weaknesses of the class or individuals that I refer to when grading for report cards.

- My lesson plans are most effective when I state goals, themes, and objectives boldly. Then I date the correlated activities as I introduce them. The difficult part of the creative dance process is that the next lesson might be to continue where I left off. If that is the situation, I clearly specify in my plan what was accomplished and the activities or direction I should focus on in the next class. For example, I may write: "The basic concept of symmetry was introduced. The students explored symmetrical shapes alone and with partners. Continue with the shapes next week and add symmetrical nonlocomotor movements."

- Before school begins I prepare a lesson plan notebook for activities. I write down the goals and objectives for each activity, the appropriate grade levels for each activity, the allotted time for each activity, and a list of equipment and where to find it. I clearly describe each activity so that anyone could pick up my notes and teach. I usually add variations to the activity in my notes. I also include the rules and procedures for the class and the weekly schedule. With this substitute notebook, I do not have to worry about writing a separate set of detailed lesson plans for every class when I am sick.

 Tip

Use a computer to develop your lesson plans. However, do find a method for maintaining your notes, and keep them with you because computers are not always available while teaching.

 Trench Truth

My lesson plan book reflects my teaching process. By the end of the year it is filled with drawings, notes, comments, and so forth. It is a workable and worked notation. If my principal wanted to see my plans, I'm sure he would be totally confused, because they don't resemble the lesson plans of a classroom teacher. No one has access to this plan, so I try to be clear for myself, because the more classes I teach the more difficult it is to remember where I am in the creative process.

Logistics of Integrated Arts

The school district where I teach provides the elementary students with 2 hours of arts classes each week. The arts classes comprise creative dance, music, and visual arts. Each class lasts 40 minutes. The time serves as a preparation period for classroom teachers. For example, three classes of fifth graders attend arts classes while their classroom teachers cooperatively plan units of study. The premise of this arts structure is to provide an environment in which the arts can be integrated without scheduling problems for the classroom teachers. The emphasis is on the relationship of elements and concepts between the arts, such as balance, rhythm, line, and shading. Another focus may be the comparison of the arts of a particular culture or time. Concepts or elements are introduced and the students then create artistic projects based on their understanding of the relationship of those concepts or elements in the different art forms.

 **Obstacle**

Scheduling

 **Solutions**

- The principal officiates over the scheduling for the entire school, but there is a scheduling team that comprises the reading specialists, the special education teachers, the media center specialist, the arts teachers, the physical educator, one or two classroom teachers, and the principal. The team examines the strengths and weaknesses of the year's schedule based on the needs of the teachers involved and on a written survey from the classroom teachers. Considering the number of students for the following year, the scheduling team brainstorms to create new possibilities for scheduling classes, recesses, and lunch periods. In establishing the schedule, the team takes great care to consider the needs of all involved.

- A scheduling goal for physical education and the arts is for the team to create a schedule that helps to eliminate the need for physical setup for each period. If the team schedules a different grade level for each period, setup consumes a great deal of time.

- When specialists have no autonomy to create their own schedule or to be part of creating a master schedule in their school, it is easy for the team to ignore certain factors that are important to these specialists. Consequently factors such as space, grade level grouping, or beneficial time periods for students might be dismissed. For example, primary classroom teachers prefer to teach reading in the morning, and therefore, they would like to schedule arts and physical education classes for the last period on a Friday. This might be beneficial for reading, but by the time the children get to their arts and physical education classes at the end of the day, they are exhausted and unable to focus on the task at hand. As an arts teacher, it can be frustrating when the scheduling team opts for this type of schedule, because it seems that the team does not regard arts education as valuable. So, I do my best to be a part of the scheduling team in order to voice my concerns and to remind others of the value in learning arts-related skills.

- Some high-risk students continuously move their homes, or their home lives are unstable. When there is a high percentage of these students in a school, it is important to have a schedule that helps them feel more secure. The scheduling team may need to adjust the length of time that primary students are away from their classroom teachers—for example, by scheduling only one arts or one physical education class a day.

- Often three or four classes of the same grade level are scheduled back to back. A difficulty for me as an arts teacher is that teaching the same subject matter can become redundant. Finding ways to keep the material fresh and alive is a challenge. Some of the advantages in repetition, however, are that by the third class I have worked out the kinks in the lesson, my presentation is clearer, and my students appear to comprehend more quickly.

 Tip

When a group of people is determining a schoolwide schedule, there needs to be a give-and-take approach that is agreeable to almost the entire faculty. But if you are on a scheduling team, remember that you can't please everyone.

Trench Truth

In elementary schools there is a tendency to set everything in stone, leaving no room for change. This is a huge problem that affects arts education. The arts activities are not games that finish with the sound of a whistle, so most of the time students are creating ideas or figuring out their course of action, and then suddenly time is up. Because students become frustrated when they can't finish an activity, and I have to begin and end my classes on time, it is important for me to pace each class with activities that can end at the designated time. I permit the students to document their work, either through drawings or writing. I save these for their next dance class. Documentation helps the students to quickly refresh their process. I also try to work out a schedule with the principal that permits some flexibility for rehearsal or performance time.

Signals for Attention

In sports, people use whistles effectively for getting students' attention. But it was not a method that I wanted to employ for dance. I tried to instill in my students that dance is a process of creating and can't be turned off and on with a whistle. I also did not want them to associate the competitive aspect of sports with the creative nature of dance. These boundaries made it challenging to find a method for getting my students' attention.

 **Obstacle**

Establishing a signal for getting students' attention in dance

 **Solutions**

- When I began teaching in the Northwest, I noticed that many music teachers had established a clapped rhythm (1, 2, 3, & 4) to

get students' attention. When the students heard the rhythm, they stopped what they were doing and echoed the rhythm. I decided to try this technique in my dance classes: I usually clap the established rhythm, or I perform a variety of sound effects with it, such as clapping thighs, vocal sounds, and other forms of body percussion. Depending on how much time there is, I expand on two to four measures of rhythm.

- Another method I have used for getting or keeping attention is to use the voice with changes in pitch and volume. After I have my students' attention, it appears that they become more focused as the volume decreases.

- I have found that a wireless microphone or a sound system with a microphone is a voice saver. The microphone wasn't my first choice for communication, because it hinders the relationship that is nurtured while dancing with my students. However, it quickly captures attention, conserves my energy, and provides a sense of calmness while helping me maintain control. When I use a wireless microphone, I have the advantage of being able to move with my students.

 Tip

Invest in a microphone that can be attached to the body or one on a headband and the sound is transmitted to a speaker system. Its benefits are priceless.

 **Trench Truth**

Teaching in a variety of situations can be very difficult. A large gym takes a toll on the vocal cords, and talking over the sounds of clanging pots and pans in the adjacent kitchen is not easy either. I once taught in a cafeteria that was used as a hallway to the gym. Besides the screams from the gym and the singing from the music room, there were ventilation blowers, mercury vapor lights, and milk coolers that blew, buzzed, and hummed continuously. There were so many noises and distractions that it was almost impossible to teach. Sound systems are in some gyms and cafeterias, and I use them to save my vocal cords. In my years of teaching, I have learned that taking care of myself is essential to being a good teacher.

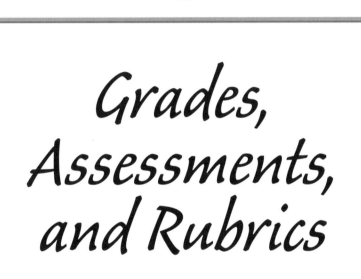

Grades, Assessments, and Rubrics

Grading System

Recently my school district developed a new trimester report card that provided a special section for arts grades. The students received two grades for each arts discipline: (1) participation and cooperation, and (2) understanding and demonstration of concepts and processes. A comment form accompanied the report card. The grades reflected the students' progress over 11 weeks of dance classes. The main difficulties with grading the arts at the elementary level are in providing grades for 900 students each grading period and ensuring that grades are fair, because grading is for the most part subjective.

 **Obstacle**

Setting grading criteria

 **Solutions**

- In my dance classes, each student scores himself at the end of each class (see chapter 3, Dance Class Management System, pages 43 through 46). These scores are part of a self-management program and become the grade for participation and cooperation. They are compiled and graded on a sliding scale for participation and cooperation.

- Understanding and demonstration of concepts and processes is the most subjective grade I have to give. When students are exploring the creative process, I take notes on their work. When students are exceptional in their creativity or demonstrate a lack of understanding of concepts, I document it in my lesson plan book or on the self-management chart at the end of the class. I refer to these notes when preparing report card grades. Exploring movement, however, is only the beginning stage of the creative process. As the trimester progresses, the students grow in how they understand and apply the elements and concepts; I consider this growth as part of the grade.

- Dance work is created in small groups (two to five students), and the product of that work is a group accomplishment. Therefore, it is difficult to know the degree that each student contributed to the dance. In order to assess individual students' progress, I spend time with each group while they are creating.

- When students go beyond the assigned criteria and demonstrate creativity beyond my expectations, they receive the highest score—a plus (+). Usually, a few students in each class receive a plus, which means that they consistently produce beyond expectations.
- If students can read and write, I use quizzes and tests on vocabulary and concepts, because they are objective tools for assessing students' knowledge.
- I test my students on dance technique to get an indication of whether they can perform specific skills.
- Sometimes I use a videotape of a project to get a concrete example of how a student performs in relation to the rest of the class.

 ## Tip

Support grades with concrete evidence; they may be challenged.

Trench Truth

In the early stages of the dance program, many students thought that dance was not important because they did not receive a grade. So I gave them pop quizzes on vocabulary, had them write essays about dance, and asked them to draw pictures to express concepts. I checked these assignments, graded them, and provided my students with comments on them. When their report cards finally included a space for dance grades, the students assumed that the subject was valuable.

Comments on Report Cards

As Martha Graham once said, "Movement never lies." Through years of experience, I have learned to read students through their dance, which reveals so much about them: their attitudes, their understandings of subject matter, their intelligence, their methods of processing information, their fears, their likes, and their dislikes.

 **Obstacle**

Finding a method for supporting grades

 Solutions

- The comment section of the report card is the most helpful, especially during the first trimester, because it awakens parents to expectations in dance education. I do not send a comment form for every child (900 students), but usually during the first trimester I comment on 150 students. On the comment section, I write relevant statements based on my observations about strengths and weaknesses, progress, behavior, creativity, or other concerns. Most classroom teachers are amazed that so much information is revealed in dance, and that it is consistent with the students' performance in the classroom. These comments are helpful to the parents and on many occasions have spurred very productive conferences.

- The comments that I put on the report card are usually brief; here are some examples:

  Amanda: Safe clothing and shoes (tennis shoes or sneakers) are required for dance and physical education.

  Vance has great creative dance ideas. He has made great improvements since last year, especially in his ability to work with others.

  Andrea is having difficulty in dance. It appears that she does not understand dance concepts, such as patterns and balance. Andrea also spends time in class chatting with friends rather than focusing on the task.

  Mary works well with others when she is focused; however, she has difficulty working alone.

Charles uses his dance time to disturb others in the class. He pushes others down and then laughs at them. When Charles is respectful to others and focuses, he does very good work.

 Tip

Find a method for communicating with parents at report card time. It gives validity to dance education, and to the content of what you are teaching.

Trench Truth

During my first three years of teaching dance in elementary school, I tried to maintain a portfolio system for each student in second through fifth grade. I filed tests and quizzes, drawings of concepts, vocabulary tests, and questionnaires of opinions and views of dance. It was a great idea, but the recording system for a transient population became too difficult. I was taking folders in and out of the file every week, only to have students return to the school before the end of the year. At that time the school had a 30 percent turnover rate; it is higher now. I discontinued this system. I found more productive ways to use my time and to document student progress, such as recording daily notes and scores; videotaping work; and grading tests, drawings, and concepts.

Rubrics

I am a firm believer in assessment, which I define as acknowledgment of the process. In assessing a student's performance, I ask these questions: Where is the student in relation to the task? What has the student accomplished? Where is the student headed? What was the student's thought process in the project? The benefits of these questions have been proven during the critique process.

 **Obstacle**

Finding a system that works for assessment

 Solutions

- The rubric method, defined as a scoring gradation of elements and concepts assigned for a project, has proven itself strong in assessing dance technique and structure. In short dance assignments, I establish rubrics with the class. After the dance is shown, it is critiqued in light of the rubric. These critiques serve as indicators of the students' ability to apply their knowledge of skills. Rubrics tend to place emphasis on specific skills and are used as building blocks to create dances that may lead to art.

- The rubric method tends to be dependent on its designer's thinking. To me, it is another method of categorizing and evaluating. It is art as a "head trip." Based on my experiences, beyond brief studies the rubric method tends to squelch feeling, self-expression, and spontaneity and prohibits ideas from moving outside the boundaries, where art is created.

 **Tip**

Explore various methods for assessing dance, such as fulfillment of rubrics, self-assessment according to rubrics, checklists filled out by students, descriptive written work, and journaling.

Trench Truth

Several years ago, a group of dance specialists organized a specific study of a task for fifth graders. We hoped that through this task we could determine how to create assessments and develop rubrics. The assessment was given at the same time of the day to all the fifth graders in the district who were involved in the study. All dance work was videotaped.

When we looked at the videotape in relation to the task, we realized that we each had a different interpretation of the directions, expectations, and results. There was much discussion and debate about the end products. We viewed the dance products and many fit the rubric, but the dance went nowhere.

Occasionally, we viewed a dance product where we unanimously agreed, "This is it; this is dance; this is creativity." But what was it? How could we put it into words? Did it meet the rubric? We agreed on when the project was successful: It was the moment when the students actually danced. It was that moment when the rubric was not the goal. It was that moment when the audience was absorbed in the movement.

Because I have such little time with each class, I can't assess every aspect of my students' performances in dance class. I have chosen to place emphasis on assessing the process and in providing opportunities where the students could experience the aha moment. The class is called Creative Dance, thus the process of creating is the focus for assessment. The aspects that *may be* the focal point in assessment are: fulfillment of rubrics, creating beyond the standards of rubrics, working as a team, written knowledge, reworking the product, ownership of the product, and so on.

Your Role As a Dance Educator

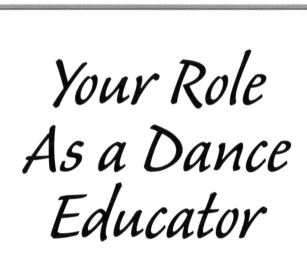

Organizing the Program

For many years as both a dance specialist and a reading specialist, I have serviced two or three schools per year and have been classed as an itinerant. In these situations, it is difficult for me to be involved with the organization of the schools and feel part of the decision-making process.

As a dance specialist and itinerant public school teacher, I have made a great effort to clearly define my role as a dance educator. The role can have three or more parts, such as (1) organization of the program; (2) communication with administration, faculty, and parents; and (3) responsibility as a teacher to the students.

 **Obstacle**

Defining your role as an organizer in the school plan

 **Solutions**

- In my role as an organizer, I assist in coordinating the classroom curriculum and the arts curriculum from which students' performances evolve.

- I facilitate the program arrangements for parent–student dance nights; informal dance showings; grade-level performances for parent viewing; and student enrichment classes (after school programs) such as basic tumbling, social and classical dance, and repertory classes.

- Serving on a school committee can have many positive effects on the school community. There are committees for team leadership, integrated curricula, school goals and incentives, faculty job search interviews, Run for the Arts or artist-in-residence programs, and arts programs. Through activities such as these, I have had the greatest opportunity to communicate with administration, faculty, and parents.

- Integrating subject matter is an effective method for developing school organization. I work with teachers to correlate subject matter and to expand on the classroom curriculum, which may evolve into performance.

Tip

If you are an itinerant teacher, choose the school or grade level where you think you can make the greatest impact, and put your energies there. The more thinly you spread yourself, the less effective you will be.

Trench Truth

Each year I service one to three schools. I need to make multiple adjustments because each school has a different philosophy and a different management system. The learning atmosphere is totally different from one school to another, and there is often a difference in the socioeconomic aspects of the population.

I carry my equipment from school to school, and I set up each space as best and quickly as I can. I must work with two or three principals and two or three faculties and an abundance of secretaries, maintenance people, and kitchen workers. The most difficult aspect of this traveling position is that I do not get an office, a desk, or a file cabinet in some situations. It is quite an adjustment, but in most schools there is no space. It has taken a lot of negotiating and outright pleading just to get a file cabinet that could be locked for confidential records. I often feel like a traveling salesman!

Communication

In my role as a dance educator I must communicate consistently and effectively with administrators, classroom teachers, staff, and parents. I have experienced several positive results from my efforts to communicate, especially the validation of arts education.

 **Obstacle**

Experiencing the results of communication

 **Solutions**

- I have noticed that arts specialists are accepted as members of the faculty when they extend themselves at all levels of communication, professional and personal.
- When I communicate consistently with others in the school and in the community, I can foster an understanding that the arts are at the core of education, rather than supplemental to it.
- I meet with teachers and parents regarding grades and student progress and to develop or enforce student behavioral plans. A rewarding result I have witnessed is that teachers and parents begin to perceive and appreciate the impact of the arts on the students.

 Tip

The sooner you realize the power of the secretary, maintenance person, and kitchen workers (if you use the cafeteria), the more effective your program will become. Take time during the first week of school and throughout the school year to acknowledge them by bringing them candy or a thank-you card and by talking with them as equals. You will find your work life much easier.

Trench Truth

One day when I was teaching, I saw students passing through the cafeteria to the gym for class. Aware of the tables and food counters that were set up, I immediately led the students away from them. The path was a little longer, but the response was worth it. The cook ran out of the kitchen to thank me for respecting her equipment. This gesture put me in her good graces, and life after that was very "filling."

Creating Goals

Education is designed for elevating the mind and for gaining knowledge of self and the world to which one relates. With this concept in mind, I have some basic goals for dance education: to provide the best dance education at that time and to those particular students, to help them experience the movement of many peoples to help them to know themselves through working with others and through experiencing critique, and to offer them a safe, nurturing environment in which to grow.

 **Obstacle**

Determining goals for fulfilling dance education responsibilities

 **Solutions**

- One goal in my classes is to create exercises for my students that tantalize their imagination. For example, "Imagine that there were no gravity. When you'd go outside for recess there would be strings holding you to the building so you wouldn't float away. Let's talk about how we could create such a dance."
- Another goal of mine is to encourage students to take risks in movement to fulfill their movement ideas. For example, "Take a chance with moving to an off-balance feeling."
- I make it an important goal to generate respect in my classes (see chapter 2).
- I direct students toward kinesthetic awareness of concepts, principles, and life.
- I try to create an environment that is safe and psychologically secure so that children feel comfortable exploring and performing dance.
- I help students internalize self-management skills that allow them to experience the joy of movement.

Tip

Maintain high goals and standards, and your students will strive to achieve them.

 **Trench Truth**

In one school in which I taught, the philosophy was that the children were great. It was true that the students were good, talented, and bright. The parents, who were manipulated by their children, affected many decisions in this school. These parents, like all parents, wanted their children treated with respect, love, and gentleness. They maintained that there was little reason for corrections or consequences. They insisted that discussions and instructions were to be in a sweet tone. Class management was to be a gentle reminder of what was expected. The arts were considered a time for fun, and the challenging of students to extend themselves creatively was not supported, especially if the students complained of difficulty, embarrassment, or partners who were unpopular. In this powerful position, the children realized that they could do anything they wanted or be excused from anything they didn't like. Common slogans were, "I'll get you fired" or "My mother will be here to talk to you."

In April, very talented fifth graders who had five years of dance were assigned a 30- to 60-second creative dance solo. This was an assignment that previous classes had fulfilled with positive results. One child who was a star in sports felt embarrassed about the project. I suggested that she create a sport dance or use the movement from different sports in her dance. Her mother was furious because she felt that her child would be too upset to perform and that it was unfair that this assignment would be graded. The parent stated that dance had no relevance to her child's development and that she would rather have a zero for a grade than force her to perform. With the consent of the principal, she took the child out of the class until the end of the year.

After this incident, the rest of the class realized that if one girl didn't have to perform a solo, they wouldn't have to perform one either. More parents called, wrote notes, or came for a conference. The principal allowed certain children whose parents were involved in the school to be exempt from the assignment. The classroom teacher began to observe the class to see if the students were being disturbed or humiliated.

After listening to the concerns, I discussed with the students their wonderful creative abilities and how they had blown the entire assignment out of proportion. I also expressed how I felt about adults robbing children of opportunities to grow, but I firmly stated that I wouldn't take away the wonderful gift that they were assigned. I tried to encourage the children to create something simple, such as walking in pathways, creating a series of shapes or directions, and so on.

The whole process became a battle of the wills—the principal's, the teachers', the parents', the children's, and mine. I didn't concede. I set a deadline for the projects and all but five students performed some type of movement to complete the assignment. The five who did not perform received a minus grade on their report cards. In retrospect, I wonder if it was really worth it. The children had gained nothing from the situation, the principal, parents, and teachers were annoyed because I set a goal beyond what they thought was appropriate, and I stressed myself out to no avail.

Teachers Are Human

Even though teachers try to function from an all-embracing, all-caring, and all-understanding criterion, we have moods and feelings. Teachers are human!

 **Obstacle**

Operating from one's emotional state

 **Solutions**

- If I am bogged down with my own emotional state, it becomes difficult to be fair and objective when dealing with students' behavior. I try to consider the following questions when working with students: Am I feeling well? Am I having personal problems? Did the previous class put me in a tense mood? Is there a child in the class who always pushes my buttons? Do I feel frustrated with the students' lack of focus or progress? If I answer yes to any of these, then I back off the students and try to stay cool!

- Being honest about my feelings is helpful in establishing class management. If I explain to the students that I am not feeling well or that I had a problem that put me in a bad mood, they will have a basis for my views or actions. Most students are sympathetic to me, and the result is usually very positive behavior.

- I speak respectfully to my students, and I expect reciprocal behavior. I rarely raise my voice or show anger toward the class (unless justified, such as when students are deliberately hurting each other). I usually wait quietly for their attention or sometimes draw their attention with silly noises while maintaining a light attitude. When students realize that I'm waiting, they settle down quickly. This method of getting their attention saves me energy from yelling, clapping, and whistling. I am, however, very firm when giving directions and corrections.

- I concentrate on being clear and not giving double messages about personal boundaries. When I make jokes or try to be comical, I usually inform my students that it is a joke. Some children are unable to distinguish between serious and humorous styles.

Tip

Be honest with yourself. Analyze classroom problems objectively—is it the students' behavior, or is it your own problem?

Trench Truth

It took me a while to realize this fact, but a teacher needs to take care of himself. If you are stressed or sick, you should stay home. I have dragged myself to teach only to realize that my patience was low; everything aggravated me; or I totally disregarded problems. My students can occasionally have a substitute, and they will appreciate me more when I return. I have had days when the students were verbally disrespectful and argued with each other, some parents complained about requirements, and the principal was unsupportive. On days like this, I take a walk at lunch and change my lesson plans to a game style for the rest of the day. In such tense situations, I find it best to keep myself calm even if it's at the expense of curriculum.

Clear Relationships

As a teacher, one area that can be most confusing is the type of relationship I have with my students. This is particularly true as a dance teacher, because dance is your personal self; it is kinesthetic; it is emotional, it is about feeling; and it is also about the way you relate with your students.

 **Obstacle**

Developing clear relationships

 **Solutions**

- I try to show my interest in students by developing their self-concepts through praise and encouragement. But if a child is particularly upset, I may quietly talk to him. Hopefully, I will be able to help if only by saying, "I can see that you're unhappy. What can I do for you?" Most children only need to know that you care.

- Because I am the teacher, I need to be clear about my relationship with each student. I am not the student's friend, buddy, parent, or grandparent. Adding these types of relationships to the teacher–student relationship intensifies confusion for young children; many take advantage of the situation while others in the class feel left out. Being fair and clear about my role as teacher can create a secure environment and eliminate troublesome situations.

- Today, many students are troubled or come from extremely dysfunctional homes. A natural response is to reach out to each child who has problems. But getting personally involved can become emotionally draining when working with large numbers of students who I teach once a week. Also, maintaining class management while having a sympathetic relationship with particular individuals could create estrangement among others in the class.

Tip

Be available to your students by offering support and kindness. However, as a dance specialist the role demands that one works closely with the classroom teachers, principal, counselors, psychologists and nurses to serve each student's needs. At times, availability means to represent the child by getting the services that could help.

Trench Truth

In my teaching situation, I work with 750 to 900 students per week. My level of involvement with my students is difficult to determine, and I must take seriously its effects. I am mostly concerned with being fair and not showing favoritism to certain students. I rarely get involved on an out-of-school, personal level with my students or their parents, because, for example, if I go to one birthday party, then I'll need to go to every birthday party. Although there are many that I care about deeply, I know that there is no way that I would be able to emotionally serve all of the students. When I am concerned about things that a particular child said, a change in mood, or aggressive or extremely submissive behaviors, I talk with the counselor, principal, or classroom teacher. They often have a broader image of the child and know the total situation. The information that I contribute solidifies my concern or brings new light to the problem.

The Teacher and the Therapist

A teacher must keep a clear perspective of her role: Is it teaching, or is it therapy? Therapy types of relationships appear to take much more time than what is allocated for a dance class. This, however, is a concern that each professional must assess for himself.

 **Obstacle**

Establishing limits

 **Solutions**

- As a director of dance for young children, I struggle with what is appropriate for their development. I am continuously evaluating who and where they are. Although I am eager to open their minds to learning, I am careful not to dump adult experiences and awakenings on them.

- The journey of dance can be deep and personal, and many students bring to it a lifetime of experiences well beyond their years. I am neither a psychologist nor a movement therapist, and I have not been trained to help them if and when they connect with the depth of their being. Although I am an educator with a desire to enrich their lives, I do not have the right to push young children down the crowded corridors of a spiritual search or personal trauma. These are children! They are not in the same place as adults who have the freedom to choose which roads they want to follow.

 Tip

Use dance to help your students develop personal control, respect for others, pride in their accomplishments, and joy in moving. Striving to reach these goals, expose your students to the power of dance, and allow it to gently touch their lives.

Trench Truth

A third-grade classroom teacher informed me that Sarah's mother had attempted suicide. It was a brief discussion, and it had almost left my mind until two weeks later. For 20 minutes before school started, I was part of a school enrichment program. One particular morning, I showed the students a video of Michelle Kwan's ice skating championship. Later during dance class, someone made a reference to the tape and began comparing Michelle Kwan to Tara Lipinski. After much discussion about which skater they liked best, I gave my opinion: "Tara Lipinski is a great skater, and she can perform wonderful jumps. But Michelle Kwan is an artist; she opens herself and expresses her feelings to the audience. Michelle skates the way I tell you to dance—open your soul and express who you are."

The students were quiet for a moment and then began to discuss breath and gentleness. Sarah timidly raised her hand and said, "My Mom's soul is very sick." Like a bolt of lightning I remembered the story the teacher had shared with me. My response was, "It is very difficult when your soul is sick, and it takes a long time to heal. You just can't put a Band-Aid® on it. Your soul needs lots of love, caring, and patience to heal." Everyone was silent for a few moments. Sarah soon smiled as if she understood and agreed.

Sarah's story is just a small indication of how dance and other arts gently take the students into great depth of feeling, and without too many words they find meaning. Her story also demonstrates how children can be supported and have their feelings validated without the dance educator being overly involved in their lives.

Taking Care of Yourself

Teaching dance to young children presents unique problems for the teacher. If you have never been with hordes of small children for long periods of time or worked in an elementary school, take heed to the information that follows.

 **Obstacle**

Staying healthy

 **Solutions**

- When working with young children, I expect to be exposed to a multitude of germs and diseases. Children continuously cough and sneeze in my face. I double or triple my dosage of whatever it is I'm taking to stay healthy—echinacea, vitamin C, bee pollen, or garlic. It is easy to become run down and susceptible to contagious diseases, especially in the beginning years.

- I take care of my voice. Laryngitis is a common ailment of dance educators. The degree of tension caused from teaching or establishing class management affects the voice. If it is necessary to yell in order to be heard in a gym, I expect vocal problems. I use a microphone.

- In the dance world taking three or four dance classes a day in addition to attending rehearsals may be a common routine, but teaching requires a different type of energy. Many children are depending on my abilities to teach, dance, and care. Parents, teachers, and administrators are also depending on my leadership in the arts and my responsibility to the students and the school. My focus is continuously distracted by the need to establish class management. My body is warmed and cooled during every class, which is difficult on the muscles and for maintaining energy. At the end of the teaching day, I may need a transition period of rest before racing off to personal classes and rehearsals. I listen to my body!

- Many dance teachers prefer wearing a leotard and tights, which are standard dance clothing. I need to take into consideration my population, how many times during the day I will go into and out of the dance space, and the distance to the bathroom. I usually wear sweat pants and a T-shirt, because it is the required clothing for the students. Sweat pants tend to be best for keeping my muscles warm. And because I am constantly warming up and cooling down, I wear a light jacket that I can slip off and on all day.

- If I were working on a raised wooden floor, I would teach barefoot. But because I'm on concrete all day, I rely on comfortable, well-fitted athletic shoes, which I hope will continue to prevent joint deterioration and tendinitis.

- I have examined elementary school faculty rooms from coast to coast, and I have found an abundance of cakes, pies, doughnuts, cookies, candy, ice cream, chips, and dips. I can easily gain 5 to 10 pounds if I eat in the faculty room, because everyone wants me to taste what he has made. The faculty room, however, is the best place to know and communicate with classroom teachers.

- When your work is kinesthetic, it is difficult not to touch people. When we are working on technique, balance, or weight share, I usually inform the students that I will be coming around to help them. For example, if I want them to tighten their gluteal or abdominal muscles, I may point to the area on my own body or make reference to a skeleton or muscle charts. Because of children's interpretation, the parents' mistrust, and the degree of sexual abuse in this country,

I must take great care to protect myself. This problem has become so much in the fore that I am conscious never to be alone with a child. If a child comes to talk with me in my office (which is a storeroom), I slowly escort the child to the gym or cafeteria and open the door to the public. I move inconspicuously so as not to bring the situation to the child's attention. I may think I know a child, but if for some reason he accuses me of inappropriate touching, it will become my word against his, and it will be my reputation or my job on the line. In an attempt to prevent sexual abuse in this country, we have swung the pendulum to the opposite extreme, and in the school setting everyone is mistrusted and questioned.

- It is a good idea to take some courses in communication, class management, and problem-solving or conflict-resolution techniques. Although I was hired to teach dance, the most challenging work has little to do with dance.

 Tip

Know your physical and emotional limitations. A limitation is not a crime; it is a fact. Take care of yourself, because no one else will. For example, if you are interested in maintaining your weight, it may be best to tell the faculty that you are prone to diabetes, have a sugar disorder, or have a dessert allergy.

Trench Truth

A new dance teacher was hired to teach dance in a middle school (sixth through eighth grades). She taught in a leotard and tights. There was nothing wrong with that. After class she continued to wear her dance clothing as she traveled throughout the school. There was nothing wrong with that, either, but students and teachers were concerned because she wasn't wearing a bra. Because this was the first time that most of the students had experienced this normal dance attire, it sent them into a dither. The situation became out of control in this rather conservative community, and eventually the teacher resigned. The moral of the story is this: Know your community, and know its boundaries. These boundaries can be expanded once people know and trust you.

The Creative
Process

Dance is many-sided
   taking on different meanings and purposes
      as you travel through the chapters of life.

Dance is a personal journey
   knowing yourself
      physically, emotionally, spiritually
         then expending the knowledge
            to express yourself
         through
            MoVeMeNt.

Dance is a driving force within a community.
   The energies of each individual caught up
      in a magnetic force
         like a black hole
            that takes us
         into
      another
   dimension.

Dance is ritual.
   It can be accompanied by pulsing rhythms
      a repetitious chant
         driving you into trance.

Dance is creation
> *yours or another's*
>> *improvised or repertory*
>>> *from a seed of idea*
>> *through the process to blossom.*

Dance is tedious hours of technique
> *released into a moment of flow*
>> *an unfaithful love affair*
>>> *that is fickle with your emotions.*

Dance is a sharing
> *an idea or a belief, a story, a concept.*
>> *It spans an array of emotion*
> *from humor to despair.*

Dance is performance.
> *It is an opening and giving of yourself*
>> *serving the laughter, tears, and thoughts of others.*

Dance is the simple joy of moving
> *laughter and happiness with each leap and spin.*
>> *Dance is*
>>> *Freedom!*

Dance takes on a variety of purposes as we travel through life. These may include the process of creating, the connection of the body and soul, an avenue to work through personal experiences, the joy of movement, the accomplishment of performance, and the challenge of competition.

It appears that there are two motivating factors for children in dance: (1) the joy of movement and (2) dance performance. The joy of movement exemplifies freedom, happiness, and a body–mind–spirit connection. In dance performance, personal gratification is acquired in the finished product and in the act of presentation. The union between performance and the joy of movement is a treasure that I strive to capture in the creative process.

The process through which one creates is similar for most artists and is learned through experience. A unique aspect of a creative dance program is that the process is the core of the program. The process can encompass the following aspects: exploring, creating, showing, critiquing, reworking, rehearsing, performing, and reviewing.

In a dance class, the elements and concepts of dance are taught, reinforced, and expanded to the many possibilities that movement offers. Students learn the methods for utilizing movements to create dances.

Part II is an explanation of the approach that I use in order to take the students through the creative process, and the other areas of life that may be explored along the way.

CHAPTER

The Creative Process: The Idea

The Exploration Stage

Exploring movement provides opportunities for self-expression and inventiveness. The movements that are explored create a base on which dance blossoms. During the exploration stage students are able to create new movements and try the ideas of their classmates. They explore the unique—that which is different from anything they have done or seen. It is a time of connection between physical and intellectual understanding.

 **Obstacle**

Getting students to express themselves and explore movement

 **Solutions**

- One method of learning is through imitation and observation. For example, I may have my students follow me in a series of straight, zigzag, or curved pathways and then discuss the movement introducing the term "pathways."

- Another method is to introduce and discuss the vocabulary of a particular concept or dance element. For example, I write the word "pathway" on the board. I ask what the word is and what it means. The students usually respond, "It is a path, road, street, trail; made of bricks, stones, dirt, cement, twigs." From this information most students establish a visual image of the word "pathway." The students then physically explore all the related possibilities of movement. As they dance, I suggest other dance elements that could be integrated in their movement.

- Another aspect of the exploration stage is to discuss how the movement feels, associate imagery with it, or create other possible descriptions. For example, after exploring curves and zigzag pathways I may ask my students how these pathways are the same or different (or I may use the terms "compare" and "contrast," which will connect to terms used in other areas of the curriculum). The usual responses are "Smooth and sharp; like a roller coaster and a knife; like a soft wind and a robot." Using their images, we continue to explore the feeling of the pathways. When the students appear comfortable with the movement, they are divided into two groups, usually by dividing the space in half. Each group dances the movement, allowing the other half to observe. Through this activity, each student demonstrates his understanding of dance concepts and gets new ideas through observing others.

- In the exploration stage, I use the term "spontaneous dance" because the movement is an immediate response to the concept that I am introducing. Spontaneous dance provides an opportunity for the teacher to observe the students' spontaneous creative ability and their understanding of dance elements and concepts. I do not use the term "improvisation" because improvisation is based on form and structure. When an artist improvises she deviates from the form, but after the improvisation she returns to the basic form or flow of the dance. In the exploration stage, the students are not aware of the form. One needs to know the rule (form) before he breaks it.

 Tip

Use correct vocabulary in written and verbal forms, which will enhance the reading process and connect to other areas of the curriculum.

Trench Truth

Although imitation and observation are two methods of learning, I am aware if that is all a student is doing. I allow students to observe each other because many children are not sure of what the assignment was or what is expected of them. However, if a child is only observing others, I attend to the child's needs to determine the problem and to help the child progress.

Many students complain that others are copying their ideas. Because this exercise is just a quick one for exploring concepts, I sympathetically respond, "I know. You'll be OK." This response ends the discussion; with it, I acknowledge the problem of both the one who copied and the one being copied.

Exploring in Teams

One of my goals for my students is to enjoy dance and to learn to express themselves through movement. There will, however, only be a few who will choose a life as dancers. For most of my students, dance classes in the public schools will terminate by sixth grade. Therefore, in addition to the joy of dance and the concepts of the art of dance, I think that the dance class offers many valuable lessons that will prepare the students for life. One of life's lessons on which I focus is learning to work with others.

 **Obstacle**

Motivating students to work with others

 **Solutions**

- I introduce the concept of symmetry as I fold a piece of paper in half and cut a simple design opposite the fold. My students discuss their perceptions of what the design could be. When I unfold the paper, a new shape appears. The students react to the new shape. In response to their ideas, I say, "It can be whatever you think it is. It is your interpretation." The emphasis is not on the interpretation of the art but on the concept of symmetry. I continue:

  Who knows what is similar about the shape? Yes, it has a fold down the center and it is the same on both sides but opposite. Does anybody know the term for this style of art design? Symmetry! The fold is called "the line of symmetry," and it is the dividing line at which the sides are reversed.

  I write the vocabulary on the board: "line of symmetry," "symmetrical," "same," "opposite," "reverse." I demonstrate a symmetrical shape with my body and say:

  The line of symmetry begins at the center of my head and continues through the center of my body. I have one eye on each side of the centerline, or the line of symmetry, one nostril and half a mouth on each side and one arm and leg on each side.

- I demonstrate several symmetrical and asymmetrical shapes. The students analyze and discuss the shapes. Many analyze the lack of symmetry because of clothing, hairstyle, or jewelry, but I point out that we are interested in the symmetrical shape of the body. The students begin to explore their own shapes and examine whether the shape is the same on both sides. Controlling the eyes is important to make the shape symmetrical. It is a challenge for the students to make their eyes symmetrical by looking forward, looking at their noses, or whatever ideas they think are possible.

- Over a period of time (one or two classes), I expand the lesson. The dancers explore symmetrical shapes at a variety of levels, symmetrical movement in their space (nonlocomotor movement), and symmetrical movement that travels (locomotor movement). They enjoy the traveling movement because opposite sides move simultaneously, which is unlike usual traveling movement in opposition. Occasionally, I call attention to someone's movement that I think is unique or interesting, in order to clarify the concept. At this point of the process, my goal is to maintain the flow and enjoyment of the exploration. I may divide the class in half to show their symmetrical shapes and movements.

- The activity continues as I choose two dancers and together they demonstrate a symmetrical shape. It is determined what the line of symmetry is between the two dancers. When the students analyze the shape, the difference in the size of the dancers is the factor that seems important to their concept of symmetry. Here is the opportunity for me to suggest that they choose a partner of similar size. This partner may not be their best friend or someone they particularly like, but it is an opportunity to work with someone "the same but different." If the number of dancers is uneven, three dancers who appear to understand symmetry are placed in a group. The idea is a little more complex because the fold, or line of symmetry, is through the center person. With a partner or group, the dancers explore symmetrical shape at a variety of levels, symmetrical movements that are in their space, and symmetrical movements that travel. The symmetrical traveling movement is mind-boggling for many because the work is in opposition. I spend time with each team helping them with the concept or with teamwork, or motivating them to expand their ideas. At the end of the exploration stage, there is a brief showing of work from each team. This may be followed by discussion and analysis of the work.

Tip

From a teacher's point of view, it is essential to be flexible in presenting dance elements and concepts. The teaching of basic dance elements and concepts can become redundant year after year and the response from the students becomes anticipated. Research and discuss with other dance specialists the many different approaches to teaching dance elements and concepts. It will increase your knowledge and develop a grab bag of different activities that will help you stay fresh and maintain personal interest in the exploration stage.

Trench Truth

Students' responses to teamwork differ depending on how long they have used teamwork. When teamwork is relatively new, several responses always seem to surface: the two may actually work well together, one child may take charge and create her own ideas, the two may say that their classroom teacher told them they are not supposed to work with each other, or the two may stand frozen or walk away from each other. My response differs depending on the class and the students involved. When there is a problem with teamwork I usually respond by saying, "You are only working with your partner for a very short time; you are not marrying him." Most of the time, the students laugh about it and then focus on the activity. A healthy competition evolves as the students begin to grow in confidence in their dance projects, especially when they think that their work is particularly unique or humorous. At this point they have moved beyond their partner concerns and have begun to focus on the quality of their work.

The Creation Stage

After the exploration stage, the creative process continues and enters the realm of choreography with meaning, form, and structure. During this stage of the process a dance or movement study springs forth or is assigned. I make a distinction between the two for clarity. In my classes the students create dances that are based on *movement studies* that focus on dance elements (pathways, level changes, directions) or a concept (balance and counterbalance). They also create *dances* that use the movement studies but have the purpose of expressing a particular idea, feeling, or story (vegetables, joy, the American Revolution).

 **Obstacle**

Finding methods for guiding students through building a dance

 **Solutions**

- Most dance projects begin with brainstorming for an idea. This method allows students the opportunity to take ownership of the dance from the beginning of the work. The students suggest ideas that I write on the board. I use a mapping technique to group the ideas. We then discuss the movement possibilities of the suggested ideas to determine what is feasible, which ideas have movement potential, and which ideas can be combined. When all ideas have been discussed, the students usually vote to determine the dance theme.

- To spur my students to create movement, I help them establish criteria for the dance. If students are working on a movement study dance, they determine the criteria that are rooted in the elements or concepts. The criteria are established for the entire class, and they are fulfilled in small groups. For example, they may decide to create a dance that demonstrates the following criteria:

  A symmetrical group shape

  Symmetrical movements that travel

  An element of surprise

  Two different pathways with level changes

If the class is working on a dance about a story, idea, or feeling, I have them divide the theme into parts. They discuss each part to determine the necessary movement ideas. Then I assign the parts or they are claimed by the group that wants to work on them. For example, some second graders created a harvest dance that was divided into vegetables, vegetable pickers, scarecrows, and crows. The students decided that the best way for expressing their ideas was with the following criteria:

Vegetables need to fall and roll.

Vegetable pickers need to pull and dig.

Scarecrows need to make shapes and surprise.

Crows need to peck and fly.

I determined the length of each part and gave them a lot of direction.

- I write these criteria on the board to serve as clarification, reference, and assistance in the critique. I stress that the dance will need to have more than the basic criteria, and each group determines the order in which they will fulfill them. When the criteria are demonstrated in the order that they are listed, the students will have a basic idea of the dance. The students quickly learn that dances are expected to include more than the required elements. I often repeat this to them: "The criteria are the bones or the skeleton of the dance. But the dance will need muscles, skin, and blood flowing through its veins to make it live."

- The students that I teach usually choose to work in a circle formation, going together and apart and under the hands of the opposite person in the circle. This movement is fine; however, I encourage my students to explore other ways of doing the same movement:

    Drop the hands and go around the opposite person rather than under her arm.

    Have two people move toward each other while the other two move apart and vice versa.

    Work the dance in a square or line formation.

    Change the level or turn the movement.

    Although I want the students to own the movement, it is sometimes necessary to plant ideas in their minds. Ideas stimulate thought!

 Tip

In the world of education, there is no one right way to do things. You will need to adjust every idea to the students—who they are, what motivates them, and what abilities and limitations they have.

 Trench Truth

After 2 or 3 minutes of work, some students announce that they are finished with their dance, and I ask to see a demonstration. Depending on the quality of work and the students in the group, I respond with my usual phrase, "That's very good, but it's only your first thought. Did you explore all the possibilities of movement?" Or I may respond with my second usual phrase, delivered in a humorous manner, "Dance is never finished; it is always growing, changing, and evolving to stay fresh and alive." The students usually look at me with scrunched up faces, and then they go back to work. My intention is not to frustrate the students but to encourage them to explore and create new and interesting movement, and not to use the same worn-out ideas.

Creating Under Time Constraints

During the choreographic aspect of the process, the objective is to create and organize the material in a unique and interesting way. I usually spend time with each group to help them organize their ideas and to keep them on task. The challenge for the students during this part of the process is that time is limited.

 **Obstacle**

Working within a required time frame

 Solutions

- The time scheduled for creating dance projects is limited. Limited time accelerates the process, and students learn to focus and use their time efficiently. When there is no time limit, students who are unmotivated dawdle without accomplishing the task. The end result of this stage of the creative process is to show work; therefore, when there is a time limit the students zoom in on the project so they will have work to show.

- Depending on the task, the time limit could be from 3 minutes to three classes. (The students, of course, do not know that the lesson will extend for three classes.) If a project is carried to the following week or is continued for an extended time period, I encourage the group to work outside the class time. I call it "dance homework," and I suggest that they come into the gym to practice during recess. Many students realize that I will be there to assist them during the recess period, and they come to take advantage of the situation.

- The length of time in which students are engaged in creating a dance is expanded throughout their years in the dance program. In first grade the students usually have a new activity each class, whereas by third or fourth grade a single dance project may continue for several classes.

- Although young students have little concept of the length of time and may not understand fully how quickly time passes, they do realize that the smaller the number of minutes available, the shorter the time they have for creating. Also, I use the intonation of my voice to imply whether the assignment is quick or extended.

 Tip

A limited amount of time tends to eliminate the students arguing with each other and spending time disliking their partners. I usually say, "We'll show the works in 4 minutes." This implies that they should hurry up.

 **Trench Truth**

Many of my students choose to spend their recess periods working on dance because they get ideas from students in other classes, and they have additional time to organize. For many it is a place safe from the social demands of recess and from unpleasant weather. They can be free to move around trying ideas and creating masterpieces with their teams. They also get a lot of personal attention. As a performance draws closer, the gym bustles with excited dancers. Students ask, "Dr. Dance, can you look at our dance? We've made changes," or "Dr. Dance, is it too late for my group to rework our dance?" or "Dr. Dance, it's raining outside; can I come in and watch the dancers?"

Grouping for Creating

I group my students in a variety of ways depending on the time allotted for the process. Usually, grouping is random, which provides them with a variety of partners. Although this method in itself can create problems, I know that in the "whole picture of life" learning to work with a variety of people is a necessary skill. Random grouping eliminates friends always working together at the exclusion of others. It can also separate the students who are lacking confidence or who are unmotivated. There are additional ideas for grouping students in chapter 5, Methods for Grouping (pages 92 and 93).

 **Obstacle**

Determining the best partner or grouping

 Solutions

- If the dance activity is extended over a period of time, I group students according to those who may benefit from working together. However, if dance projects are developed during one class period, I may put students together who usually avoid each other, who may have difficulty working together, or who are of the opposite sex. These groupings challenge my students to find a method beyond their personal feelings to solve a problem.

- With emphasis on teamwork, the students collaborate to bring their ideas to fruition. Some may have many ideas and progress quickly. Others tend to say nothing, argue, or look around at others, hoping to get an idea from them. Groups who think that they have a great idea learn to work quietly so as not to draw attention to their masterpiece. This technique developed so that other groups couldn't steal their ideas.

- In grouping, one of the most common difficulties is that one person wants to be the boss, telling the others what to do, and she upsets the rest of the group. In this situation, I take the group to examine the required criteria written on the board. I assign or allow each student to choose one part of the criteria that he will create. Then each works on that task. After a minute, each student in that group demonstrates the movement. I help them to decide as a group the order of each movement that they will do in unison. When I think that they have a handle on the situation I walk away to let them create, regroup, or add movement that enhances the project. My intervention is only necessary once, twice, or in some cases for the entire school year; afterward, the students work it out themselves.

- Another problem is disruptive behavior of a team member. If one student is having difficulty cooperating or staying focused, I will work with the group for a while until the student is on task. I rarely remove a child from group work. Many times, students refuse to cooperate because they want to be removed.

 Tip

If the population is extremely transient, problems occur in extended dance projects. The group is always starting over with new students, and the flow of the idea is lost. In this case, focus on short dance studies that can be accomplished in one class.

 Trench Truth

In preparing my students for life I explain the following:

> Not all teachers will take the time to prepare you for life situations, but I will. When you leave school I want you to be prepared to meet the challenges that life will offer. It may be difficult to prepare yourself, but very soon you will have a job. One of the hardest things about a job is getting along with others. If you go to the boss and say, "I don't want to work with John," the boss will say, "Fine, you're fired." And if you go to another job, there will be others there that you also don't like or get along with. You will need to determine what to do. Do you learn to tolerate others and perhaps end up working well with John or do you end up without a job, money, and the necessary things of life? So when I put you with a partner that you don't particularly like, think to yourself: I don't like this situation, but Dr. Dance is giving me an opportunity to get past my dislikes and figure out how to accomplish the work.

Gender Effects on Creating

It is apparent in organizational techniques and in the manner of processing information that boys and girls are different. Observation of students throughout the creative dance program revealed that boys appeared to have immediate creative ideas to explore, covered a large amount of space, appeared to display a great amount of physical energy, moved quickly, worked with high and low ranges of space, took physical risks, involved others to display their creations, approached the presentation of the work with confidence, and tended to organize ideas quickly and at the last moment. Girls, on the other hand, tended to work in a limited space, moved in a middle range at a slow-to-moderate tempo, did not take as many physical risks, and spent a considerable amount of time in the organization of the movement. These differences between boys and girls can bring about difficulties in grouping students and in the way they create together.

 **Obstacle**

Being aware of processing differences between genders

 **Solution**

Tracking the manner in which the students process information and create dances allows one to see the differences and the progress. After several years in the creative dance program in which my students experienced and observed a lot of dance, there was a definite difference in their approach to creating: The boys continued to have great difficulties in working out their ideas with the girls. They felt creatively suppressed with all the organization and the lack of full movement. They also thought that the girls wouldn't listen to their ideas. The boys were able to focus on intricate movements that required rhythmic beats. The girls were observed moving with confidence and attempting movement that displayed creativity—something out of the ordinary. They displayed movement that changed levels and had occasional changes of energy.

Tip

The earlier the children learn to work in mixed-gender groupings, the less difficulty they will encounter when they enter puberty; it will be a matter-of-fact situation for them. Don't avoid mixed-gender groupings, because you will not be helping your students that way. You need to offer much guidance to support the students while they process their differences and to assure that each student feels included in the creative process as they learn to create in mixed-gender groups.

 Trench Truth

One year I worked with a group of intellectually gifted fifth graders. Their manner of embracing the work was a total pleasure. They requested to work in groups larger than five students. I agreed, and they divided themselves into three groups. The groups consisted of nine boys, nine girls, and a group of four boys and five girls. We determined the theme and the criteria for the dance. The nine boys worked as a team with a central focus but with many different parts to the dance project. They tended to frame each other—as some moved, others paused. The energy of their movement was quick and light, and their approach was clever and humorous. The group of boys and girls collaborated and focused on unison work with an interesting movement of lifting one student over their heads. The energy of their movement was intense, and it was relatively slow. Their theme was about death, and it was cleverly choreographed. The group of nine girls ran into many barricades. From the beginning of the work, the girls argued about who was in charge, they paired with their friends at the exclusion of the group, and they said many unkind things to each other. They divided into two groups to no avail. Eventually, I randomly divided them into groups of three. Two groups were able to create some basic movements. But the third group was so annoyed with the situation that they did nothing unless I guided them through the process. They did create 16 beats of movement, which was walking and making a shape. The process took two class periods and provided a very interesting study on gender. The students decided to put all the parts together and to perform it for a districtwide dance gala. The students learned a lot from the process, but they never asked to work in large groups again.

Showing the Dance

When students show their dance projects they have an opportunity to take ownership of and pride in their work. It is their own dance project, and they are primarily responsible for its outcome. As students begin to realize that dance is *more* than fulfilling the required criteria, the dance projects begin to exhibit unique or surprising accomplishments. These showings also provide an opportunity for students to draw on the ideas of their classmates.

The dance showing is also a method for testing the students' application of dance elements and concepts in their choreographed works, and for determining the following: Do they demonstrate knowledge of the elements and concepts of the dance? Are they able to complete the task? Do they remember the sequence of the movement? Do they organize the material with smooth transitions? Do they fulfill the requirements of the criteria? Do they go beyond the criteria to create interesting dances?

 **Obstacle**

Preparing the students to feel comfortable while showing dance projects

 **Solutions**

- In first grade I encourage my students to explore movement and share their ideas with the group. One activity that has been helpful in introducing the students to dance showings is Mary Joyce's The Good-Bye Dance (Mary Joyce, 1980, *First Steps in Teaching Creative Dance to Children*, Mountain View, CA: Mayfield Publishing Company). One by one the students dance across the space with their own movement while incorporating the dance element that was studied during the class. The students travel through the space alone or with a partner. They hold a shape when they have completed their dance and the audience (other students) applauds. When all the students have danced, I dance with them until the music is completed, or we may form a connected shape to end the dance. This activity provides many opportunities for the children to feel good about their movement creations and allows them time to become comfortable dancing for an audience.

- I begin having students show their dance projects in first grade. There is an understanding that everyone will present a dance project, which is a mind-set that can be easily and joyfully established at an early age. Most assignments are shown even if they are only 8 beats of movement. No one is exempt from the dance showing. But on rare occasions I excuse some children when I think that the activity will have negative or traumatizing results. Occasionally, some children may start to cry, freeze up, or tense their bodies; others may approach me with panic on their faces. These children may be excused from showing the first time. But if they repeat this behavior, I may dance with them or ask them to choose a partner.

 **Tip**

As a dance educator, you must be able to discriminate when a little encouragement would help a child to perform and when the experience could be damaging to him.

Trench Truth

When I first began teaching in the dance program, dance showing was a huge concern for my students. They were overwhelmed with inhibitions, but I gently and carefully took them down the path, assuring them at every step of the way. Now the students have seen others perform, they know the routine, and they look forward to their performance opportunities. For example, in January Jennifer's dad came to speak with me about her total fear of the dance class. Jennifer was in first grade, and her dad felt that the dance class was causing stress for his child. He wanted her to be excused from the class. I told him I wasn't aware of the problem but would help her along the way. He agreed to give her a little more time in the class. Knowing that her dad had talked with me, Jennifer burst into tears when we got to the Good-Bye Dance. She said that her dad said she didn't have to do it. I didn't insist, and she stood by the wall during the dance. The next week, I took her by the hand and skipped across the dance floor with her. The following week she danced across with her best friends. Each week it got a little easier for her.

With a gentle understanding of her need, I was able to provide Jennifer with a secure feeling about herself in the dance class. In May the first graders performed for their parents. Jennifer was out there smiling and popping up as a tulip. Her fears were overcome, and her dad beamed with pride.

When to Show the Work

There are many opinions about children showing their dance projects. Many dance educators let the children decide if and when they show their work. Others wait until a dance is perfected before they perform for an audience. In my school district, the arts teachers are expected to present performing arts programs. If all the children do not get an opportunity to perform their dance, parents become quite upset, especially if their child's class is not chosen to dance. I put emphasis on performing no matter how minimal the dance is (see chapter 10, Putting Creative Dance in the Spotlight, pages 208 through 210).

 **Obstacle**

Motivating students to perform

 **Solutions**

- Throughout the first through fifth grades, students experience many activities that prepare them for performance. It begins with the Good-Bye Dance in first grade. Students then get to experience performing their work with the class divided in half or in quarters. In these settings there are so many children dancing that usually no one fears the embarrassment of being seen by others or making a mistake. When the children are comfortable with these experiences, two or three groups or pairs of students show their work simultaneously. Eventually each group or pair of students shows their projects, and the others become the audience. This experience is coupled with applause and praise for their focus, teamwork, and ideas. It needs to be a positive experience, or children will decide never to do it again.

- At times, I videotape my students' dance showings, and later I show them the videotape as a learning experience and so that they can see how wonderful they are. For many this can be a motivating factor. Whenever I videotape them, I tell students that I will choose parts of the videotape to show at the next dance teachers' meeting or that I will feature different parts at the next conference I attend. These ideas are motivating to most children.

- When the class period is nearing the end and the classroom teacher comes to get the students, I ask whether they would like to show their work to the teacher. Young children, who are so eager to please the classroom teacher, usually respond positively. When they have performed, I encourage the teacher to address the whole class with comments about their work.

Tip

To encourage a love of performance in your students, provide a slow and secure process of exposing them to the idea of showing their dance projects.

Trench Truth

The chemistry of one third-grade class was truly wonderful; it was beyond words. There were rarely problems with cooperation. Actually, the stronger students would patiently choose and assist the weaker ones. The students loved to create dances, and when the criteria for the dance were set the students eagerly and enthusiastically began to work. By the end of the class they were ready to show their work.

One day, like many other days with this class, the students were working in five groups of five students. The music began and I was immediately drawn into the first group's work. The second group performed and I felt the passion of their dance as emotions rose inside me. By the third group I felt tears welling in my eyes. They streamed down my face by group four. Then I "lost it" as the last group performed. When they finished dancing, the class gathered around to see whether I was all right. I could only say, "You were so beautiful. You danced from your souls. I'm so proud of you." They felt really good about themselves and compared me to their mothers who cry when they do something that makes them proud.

How to Show the Work

In the creative mind, there is no magical formula to follow that would suggest a step-by-step process for showing work. Sometimes you start at the bottom and jump up two steps, or you may go down three steps and up four. But for the purpose of discussion I have included some of the methods that I use to show dance projects. Several times during the creating stage, students have a showing of their work, called Works in Progress. The order is flexible and the process depends on each class.

 **Obstacle**

Determining when the work is ready to show

 **Solutions**

- After the students have taken time to discuss and move the ideas that might meet the required criteria, I have every group perform their work simultaneously. This allows me to quickly assess their progress by asking, Are there major problems, or do the students have the general idea about the dance project? Later in the process, each group receives a space to dance in the room and a number order for performing. The groups dance according to the number order, allowing an 8-count transition between groups. It is a quick overview of their accomplishments. I usually give general suggestions or specific compliments after all the students have danced. These little dance showings help students evaluate their progress and allow others in the class to get ideas. When students demonstrate little or no progress, they are invited to join me at recess, when I am able to give them individual assistance. Many of these students think that they are privileged. The ones who think otherwise learn to use their class time more wisely.

- When the dance project is completed, the students show their work to the class. Finished projects last approximately 30 to 90 seconds. The dance showing is set up as a performance. I establish boundaries for the stage by using the painted lines on the floor or by using safety cones to divide the space. The dancers are usually watching the members of their group and concentrating on the dance. There is very little contact with the audience, unless a group tries to perform a comedy dance. After their showing, each group receives a critique about their project (see Critique Stage, pages 157 through 158).

- The dance showings have a serious tone, because I want the students to know that their work is of value and not to be taken lightly. The process of showing and performing develops slowly as other aspects are added throughout the years.

- Often there are children who are disruptive during the creative process. These students may be unfocused or playing around rather than working. After a few months (or a few years), the class is able to distinguish between work that is disruptive behavior and work that is good dance exploration. I have noticed that when the students are at this point (usually by second grade), they will not tolerate any disruptive or silly behavior when they show dance projects unless the dance is a comedy.

- I refresh or introduce relevant performance rules before the dance showing (see appendix A). Here are some of those rules and my reasons for having them:

  Beginning: The students must begin in a still shape. The shape may be on the stage area, or it may be a still position in the wings waiting for an entrance cue. Stillness demands that the students are focused and in control. For those who are going to enter the dance space, they learn to stand still and focus while in the imaginary stage wings. I suggest that they hold the seams of their pants so that their hands are under control. I have been amazed at how well the students are able to control themselves; even those who are diagnosed with attention-deficit/hyperactivity disorder (ADHD) are able to demonstrate control. When the students are cued, the dance begins.

  Middle: Although the minimum work is for the dance to fulfill the criteria, the expectation is that each dance project is unique and has smooth transitions. The students should demonstrate that each member of the group knows what to do. The efforts of the team should be evident. Many times, the creativity and ingenuity are beyond expectations; and as a result, the required criteria may lose their emphasis with an aha moment (see chapter 6).

  Ending: When the dance is completed, the dancers either freeze on stage or exit the dance space. The freeze must be held long enough to signal to the audience that the dance has been completed. When the dancers are frozen, the audience applauds. The dancers bow.

 Tip

Encourage your students to make adjustments to their dance projects. Making adjustments is an important skill to learn, because adjustments are required in performance and in life.

Trench Truth

During the first few years, the students always had an excuse for not being able to show their work. Some even found reasons for not creating: "We can't do our dance because Johnny is absent." The first time a class uses this excuse I sit them down for a little make believe:

> Your dance troupe was hired to perform at Carnegie Hall, and each dancer is going to be paid $100,000. If you tell the manager that you can't dance because Johnny is absent, he will tell you, "Good-bye." None of you would get paid and you'd probably never be asked to dance at Carnegie Hall again. What do you think you should do if someone is absent? [Usually someone responds, "Do it without him."] Yes, you'll need to readjust the dance so that it can be performed and you can get paid.

There are only a few occasions when it is necessary to remind them of this story. Most of the students understand and quickly learn to adjust their thinking.

The Critique Stage

The arts hold meaning, but they are also open to interpretation. This duality is facilitated between the artist and observer. Early in the creative process, student artists become aware that the arts support this duality and that the splendor of the arts lies within the freedom of interpretation.

In dance education the critique experience begins early and is twofold. The objective viewpoint is to critique the criteria or required elements of the work. This exercise develops focus and observational skills for the audience. The critique also offers an opportunity for students to express their opinions and interpretations that are grounded on facts, feelings, or other evidence about the dance project.

The dance project is critiqued as part of the dance showing. The critique gives the students insight into their work. If the dance project is going to be extended into a performance piece, the critique is used as a guideline to rework their projects. It appears that critiquing the work for children at this time is more valuable than after the major performance, when there is no opportunity to make changes or improve the work.

 **Obstacle**

Critiquing without ganging up on the performer

 Solutions

- The blossoming of a dance critic or dance audience requires much guidance. It is essential that I build an environment of trust and support for the creative process. I direct my students as to how to give and receive critiques. No student should feel as if the critics are ganging up on her. If respect for the efforts of others is a value, it needs to be demonstrated, and students will need to be guided in order to internalize that value.

- Early elementary school students should begin the critique stage of the creative process with a positive experience. As students mature, I guide them in developing skills that require giving and receiving of critiques that discuss the positive qualities and the need for improvement. Through critique the students receive gentle feedback about the reality of their work. Dance projects are analyzed and can be reworked after the critique. Ideas are brought to fruition throughout this stage of the process, and students are able to take pride in their strengths and acquire an awareness of areas that need to be developed.

 Tip

Be gentle and flexible in your critiques. The egos of young children are fragile, and you must always consider the maturity level of each class.

Trench Truth

I taught a course on creative dance for classroom teachers. There was much debate on the critique aspect of the creative process. Many teachers thought that it was a humiliating situation that left a child exposed and vulnerable. Some said that when they were children their artwork was criticized and as a result they never drew again. Others thought it was psychologically harmful and that no child should be inflicted with this practice.

I apologized to them for their negative experience and stressed that knowing the strengths and weaknesses of your work is what helps you to improve. No one should be humiliated. The process of critique should be affirming. Each dance work will have wonderful parts that are praised. The other part of the critique will be a map of possible roads to take for improving the work. The emphasis needs to be on the work, not on a person's ability. How you deliver a critique is vital for progress.

Critiquing in the Primary Grades

Through the Good-Bye Dance (see Showing the Dance, pages 149 through 151), children are exposed to an audience of their peers. After each student performs, the class applauds. I might occasionally add, "I really liked the unique movement that Tyron performed. I have never seen anything quite like that." Other times, I may bring their attention to a movement's quality, style, tempo, or other interesting elements. The students begin to be aware that in dance there are many options and that diversity is valued.

 **Obstacle**

Introducing the delicate stage of critique

 **Solutions**

- By the middle of their first-grade year, students are introduced to criteria critiques (even though they are not referred to by that name). The students create dance studies that specify the criteria, such as ABAB (for example, A = 8 beats of locomotor, or travel; B = 8 beats of nonlocomotor, or movement in personal space). I have them work in pairs and instruct them to work in unison. Although the students have worked with partners, it is usually their first effort of showing dance projects in unison. When the study is completed, the class audience sits quietly in a large circle with the showing of dance work in the center. I instruct the audience to look for the pattern and to count the 8-beat phrases aloud. (Not only does this activity reinforce the beat, but it also engages the audience.) After each pair performs, the audience applauds. Then I ask, "Did you see an ABAB pattern?" If there was no pattern, I may ask the dancers about their intention or to repeat instructions. Then I ask the audience, "Did each part have 8 beats?" If the dancers were off on the phrasing, they are instructed to do it again as I count for them and instruct them accordingly. Through questioning the dancers find success in their first attempt, or they experience success as they redo the work. Whenever dancers redo their work, I immediately bring their attention to the work and not to their intelligence, nor to a lack of cooperation or motivation. I praise and encourage them throughout the redoing of their work, and the audience gives them applause at the end. Through this experience everyone in the class learns that to redo the work is all right, and in fact it is expected.

- Another method for developing the critique and attention to movement is to have the students rate the frequency of the movement. For example, I give primary students a paper on which they draw three columns. At the top of each column, they draw the dance element of focus, such as curve pathway (curve line), zigzag pathway (zigzag line), or straight pathway (straight line). I assign each student a partner. When one partner moves through the pathways, the other makes a tally mark in the appropriate column. After 30 to 45 seconds, the dance ends, and they count the number of marks. Students change roles and continue the observation. Afterward, the students discuss the tallies and the movements that they observed. Both the dancer and the observer develop the ability to focus. This activity creates a kind atmosphere in which children can become aware of their inherent style of movement.

- The students also experience an opinion critique. After they have explored a dance element, I divide the class in half. Each half performs a spontaneous dance based on the explored element. When they have completed the dance, the dancers receive their applause. Then I ask the audience what was interesting to them. The students take turns expressing themselves using phrases such as "I like the way John did . . . " or "I thought Mary's jump was exciting. . . ." The critics are encouraged to support their ideas with reasons. If a student says, "I thought it was good," I'll ask what was good about it or what he really liked about the dance. Sometimes I ask the dancer to repeat the movement or to discuss how she got the idea for the movement. It is rare when negative comments are permitted; the tone is about affirming the dancers' movements that are interesting and unique, not about criticizing.

- In second grade I continue and expand the critique stage of the creative process. I use a method shared with me by Betsy Claassen, a dance educator in Vancouver, Washington, called "Three Stars and a Wish." In this method, the audience is encouraged to find three great things or three things that can be starred in the dance and then one wish for something that could improve the dance. This method encourages positive critiques and offers the children an opportunity to think about other possibilities for dance.

Tip

For young children, emphasize enjoying and exploring movement. I suggest only introducing the critique in the primary grades. Allow the students to participate in only one or two criteria critiques and opinion critiques each year. Redoing the work should be minimal and basically for clarification only.

Trench Truth

The beautiful part of primary grade critiques is that the children watch their friends and talk about how wonderful they were. The common critiques are: "I thought they were really good." "The whole thing was wonderful." "I liked it all."

By the end of first grade, I start to teach them how to critique by asking them questions such as, "What did you like about it? What was good about it? What was your favorite part? What did you think about the beginning? The end?"

Critiquing
in the Elementary Grades

Third through fifth graders choreograph and perform small-group dance projects throughout the school year. These projects may be developed in one class or over an extended period of time. They are structured according to particular criteria determined through discussion with the students and will be critiqued at the end of the project.

 **Obstacle**

Understanding the value of critique

 **Solutions**

- In third grade when the students are prepared to show their dance projects, I introduce the role of the dance critic. I have the class sit on a designated painted line on the gym floor, which I refer to as the critic's box. Then I tell the following story:

  Welcome to the critic's box. Does anyone know what a critic is? (Occasionally someone will say it's like Siskel and Ebert [movie critics who were popular in the 1990s].) A critic is someone who gives her opinion on dance, movies, ice skating, food, and so on. It is only one person's opinion; you can agree or disagree with it. However, in the dance world a critic can be responsible for your career. For example, if this class were a professional dance company, a dance critic may come to see your performance. Afterward she may write a critique in the newspaper or make a report on the television, radio, or Internet. Here's an example: "Last night the Kids Dance Company performed the most dazzling dance that I have ever seen. The dancers were focused and they danced with full-out energy. There was a clear, slow beginning, which was contrasted by exploding surprises. All the dancers were committed to the movement, which made the audience feel as if they were dancing too. If you want a most pleasant experience, then attend their performance this weekend." If this is the critique that is written about you, many people will come to the concert, and you'll make a lot of money. But what would happen if you received a critique that said, "Last night I attended a disorganized concert by Kids Dance Company. The dancers were so distracted that by the end of the dance they forgot what to do. In one part two dancers were arguing about

their place in the line and another was yelling out directions. The dance needed to be rehearsed and the dancers needed to learn to focus." If this were the critique of your performance, people would not come to the concert, and you would not make any money. The role of a dance critic is very important. You will learn to be a critic, but be gentle! If you are disrespectful to your classmates, they will probably be the same to you. Our first lesson will be to find good things about the dance. You may say, "I liked the change of tempo in the dance." Or if you like the way one person in the group moved, you may say, "I like the way some of the dancers changed directions quickly."

This story prepares the students for the critique experience.

- After each dance work, I instruct the dancers to remain in the dance space and listen to the critique. If the criteria of a dance are questioned, the dancers may demonstrate and explain areas in which they fulfilled the criteria. However, in the opinion critique I suggest that the dancers just listen, because opinion is just the way one person thinks; it doesn't make something right or wrong. Most students want to defend their movements or present their intention for their dance. I allow them to do so after the class gives their interpretations.

Tip

Dance critics are required to give reasons to support their suggestions, opinions, and interpretations. Require your students to do the same; it will develop their ability to respond clearly and to not just say anything that comes to mind.

Trench Truth

In the first year that I worked with students on critiquing, I found the process to be extremely revealing. My students, especially the girls, were brutal to each other with short, stabbing comments. They wanted to criticize everything that others did: "I didn't like the way Jannetta played with her hair; Kristin didn't do anything right; Shawnisha was on the wrong foot; Erizza was the best in the group." My objective for the exercise was for the students to focus on the dance as a whole and to respond to the dancers as a team. I found myself on edge, editing almost everything they said. Many students didn't want to show their work for fear of criticism. I stressed, "The critique should not be about your best friend or about finding fault with someone you don't like; nor should it be a vicious attack on anyone. Remember that each of you will have a turn to be critiqued. If you are brutal to others, wait until you hear what will be said to you." The class quickly established a new critique format, and the dance critics were to positively comment accordingly: "I liked the way . . . because . . . ; Most of the dancers did . . . which I thought was . . . ; The dance was . . . because . . . ." The new approach helped the students begin to change their focus. I don't know whether it was because they were clear and positive or because they feared a malicious critique about their work.

Clipboard Critiques

During the early years of the program, I introduced a written critique for informal grade-level showings where two to four classes performed their dance projects. This occurred once or twice a year as I struggled to get the students involved in the dance program. My purpose for written critiques was twofold: to develop focused audiences and to develop students' awareness of the criteria that were expected in performance.

 **Obstacle**

Making students aware of expectations, or criteria

 **Solution**

The students were given a critique form (see figure 8.1) that listed each class on the program. The first time they did a written critique it

---

Mrs. Smith's Class

Were the dancers quiet while dancing?	1	2	3	4	5
Were the dancers focused on the dance?	1	2	3	4	5
Were the dancers still while waiting at the beginning and end?	1	2	3	4	5

Draw or write about your favorite part of the dance.

Figure 8.1

addressed three criteria that I hoped would establish necessary characteristics for performance: quiet (students couldn't talk or discuss while performing, unless it was a dance that required speaking), focus (thinking about what they were doing), and stillness (beginning and ending the dance with stillness). Each student, who was a performer and observer, had to complete the form at the end of each dance. The students had to rate the dancers with 5 as the highest. I also asked them to describe or draw a picture of the most interesting part of the dance. The title Clipboard Critiques developed because the first time the students executed the exercise they arrived with their critique forms attached to clipboards and their pencils resting on their ears. They were serious about the activity and took the actions of a reporter or dance critic.

Tip

There are many ways to critique a dance project for young students. The most important principle is to be conscious of the tender egos that are trying to please you.

Trench Truth

The wonderful aspect of becoming an artist in any discipline is the immediate feedback. One receives opinions from others that can be used to develop artistic endeavors. These opinions may address areas such as the form and composition, the uniqueness of the idea or story, the quality of mood and expression, what worked or didn't work for the viewer, or the inner self that emerges in the work. The feedback is not always praise of one's strengths, because growth develops from understanding and attempting to improve the weaknesses. When the artist learns to appreciate the critique as a means of improvement and not as a personal attack, the artistic work soars.

The Process Continues: Performance

Reworking

The concept of reworking is integral to the creative process. When writing an essay, one begins with an outline, proceeds to a rough draft in the creating stage, then writes and refines several times before the essay is ready to be shared. The process of creating dance is similar. The outline is the criteria; the rough draft develops during the creating stage; and the movement is completed, refined, and finally shown and critiqued. The students then have the opportunity to rethink the dance project, analyze whether the work actually did what they wanted it to do, and consider whether they have gotten better ideas during the process. Reworking is the next option in the creative process.

 **Obstacle**

Doing it again

 **Solutions**

- On most occasions, the reworking stage of the process can be quickly handled during the dance showing and critique. I guide my students through the reworking of a dance to meet the criteria and to ascertain their knowledge of the skills. If the dancers are off beat or unclear of the phrasing, it can be counted and reworked at that time. If the dancers are not clear about the sequence, direction, or movement, the student audience can help in reworking during the critique.

- Occasionally groups rework their projects because they did not meet the criteria for a variety of reasons.

- When most of the students do not understand the objective of the project or the instructions, I realize that it was probably my lack of clarity during the explanation. I usually drop the idea and try it later through another approach.

- When a dance project will be performed for an audience other than the rest of the class, my students enter the reworking stage. This reworking stage for an audience occurs once or twice a year. During this stage, the movement may be reordered, groups may work simultaneously, and additional material could be added or deleted (see Informal Grade-Level Program [pages 191–193] and Preparing for the Formal Performance [pages 194–196]).

Tip

If children were asked to rework every product, they would lose interest and feel beaten down by the process. Be selective about what you ask them to rework.

 Trench Truth

One year I had a fourth-grade class who made little progress in the creative process. They argued within their small groups for several classes about a minimal entrance movement for a Lewis and Clark theme. Each week they changed their ideas and the arguing resumed. Finally, each group in the class agreed on the movement and they rehearsed it to preserve it. The five groups entered consecutively, which took 30 seconds. Finally! I was so pleased with their accomplishments. Then, I enthusiastically asked what they wanted to do next. Their response was, "Bow!" For this particular class, they had reached their limit. I choreographed the rest of the dance myself, and they were content to perform it.

Reworking
According to the Critique

In the elementary grades the students critique their work and begin to take ownership of their projects. They occasionally revise or rework their dance projects based on their own ideas and the information they received during the critique. The students may be given a class period and additional recess periods if they want assistance, depending on the purpose of the work. The intention is to reevaluate the work and improve the project.

 **Obstacle**

Finding the problems

 **Solutions**

- I consider the information received during the critique: Was it clear to the audience? What did the audience really like? What parts did students think needed to be reworked?
- I also focus on helping students smooth out transitions so that the dance is seamless: one movement flowing into the other, or movement that shows clear contrast.
- I help them develop clear movement cues that may be clicks, snaps, or musical phrasing, such as three stomps and jump; 4 beats and the next person starts; or a verbal cue of clicking signals, then fall.
- In the primary grades I usually signal the students' movement cues with two taps of the claves. These are executed with the musical phrasing so as to be obvious to the students but not to the audience.
- I determine the sequence of the movement: If the dancer is lying on the ground at the end of the phrase, can he begin to run on the next beat? I might ask them to rearrange the sequence so that one movement is able to flow into the next. I attempt to help them realize that the movement combinations may not be compatible (for example, trying to run from a lying position).

Tip

Be aware that some children have struggled to complete the project. The reworking stage may just be a rehearsal or a tightening up of what they have accomplished. You may need to provide these students with much guidance.

Trench Truth

When introducing the reworking of various aspects during the creative process, I tell the following story:

> My friend Maria Fama is a writer of short stories and poetry. One time she told me that she writes her stories as the ideas come into her mind. She doesn't stop to check spelling, to look up words, or to see whether the grammar is correct. But Maria said that when the story is finished, the real hard work begins. She takes out her writer's toolbox and begins to fix the parts that don't work. She tightens the loose parts, moves things around, smoothes out the rough edges, and polishes the finished product. Dance requires the same process. We put our ideas together quickly. We show the work and get feedback from the critique. Now, it is time to get out the dancer's toolbox and refine the project. It's time to think about the critique an decide what suggestions or ideas could make the dance better.

Reworking for a Performance

My students are involved in both formal and informal performance opportunities every year. The informal performances are usually part of a grade-level showing in which all classes in the same grade level perform for each other, their teachers, and possibly the principal. I think of the informal performance as a time when most of the audience has been involved in the creative process. It puts all presenters in the same learning experience. The formal dance performances have a common theme and are for the school, parents, and community. From my experience, I know that the benefits of student performances are phenomenal and are definitely worth the time and energy that go into the experience (see Informal Grade-Level Program [pages 191–193] and Preparing for the Formal Performance [pages 194–196]).

After the critique, my students enter the reworking stage of the creative process for both informal and formal performances. When the students know that they will perform their work, most become extremely involved. It's at this level that students demand high-quality work from each other. They focus on the strengths and weaknesses of the dance and find solutions to improve it.

 **Obstacle**

Putting eight projects into one

 **Solutions**

- When I set up the work for an informal grade-level performance, I try to feature the students' projects that were reworked after the critique. These projects are usually movement studies on the concepts and elements of dance. Because each class may have six to eight small groups to perform and there will be a time limit on the performances, I often have two to three groups dance simultaneously.

- A simple method for integrating the work into one dance piece may include the following steps: The class enters the dance space together and performs several unison movement phrases. Then each small group performs individually or simultaneously with another depending on the length and complexity of the projects while the other students maintain a shape or background movement. Finally, the class repeats the group movement and ends together with a bow. This is a basic style of choreography that teaches the students that they are all part of the dance and support each other with their projects.

- If the students are dancing a story theme, the structure of the dance has a different format. This is one method that I have used: A third-grade class danced the 1954 Dr. Seuss' *Horton Hears a Who.* I grouped the class for the creating stage, and each group prepared a four-page section of the book to highlight the story line. After the students created and critiqued each project, the students worked out transitions of entering and exiting. There were different students performing the characters for each section. The text was read to music with 3/4 waltz time. At the end of the story, the class took a bow.

- The possibilities for blending movement groups are endless. During the first attempt I try to be clear and directive so that the students are not frustrated by the procedure. Once they understand the possibilities, I may suggest, "I wonder how it would look if this group did such and such while that group did . . . ." I encourage the students who are observing to give suggestions. We discuss the dancers' efforts or energies, decide together whether it worked or didn't work, whether it improved the dance, whether it created something new and interesting, and whether it expressed our intention. Depending on the abilities of the students, the small group projects may be expanded so that they juxtapose each other while other projects use repetitive movement themes to interweave the parts of the dance.

Tip

Not all classes are ready for or interested in juxtaposition, canon form, or repetition as choreographic techniques. Work at the students' pace. The challenging activities should foster excitement, not dread.

Trench Truth

My Wonderland class (as described in the prelude) was capable of integrating complex movement. After creating group works, I broke up their movement studies and inserted phrases of their group movement throughout the dance. Parts of the movement were reversed or repeated or served as a thread running through the dance. There were moments of unison work and canon form. Theme and variation could be identified in the work. It was a choreographic experience similar to working in a dance company. Being involved in their development was extremely satisfying. But believe me, these moments where an entire class is focused and motivated to that point are rare.

Restructuring

As time progresses and the students become more knowledgeable about choreography, the methods of structuring dance and combining dance movements will offer endless possibilities. Learning to coordinate the movements of the smaller projects into one dance piece is a difficult process. Many of the students think that their small group project is wonderful, and they don't want to lose their masterpieces through rework and restructure. In those situations, I usually honor their place of development and choose a basic structure in which to present all dance projects.

If the students are committed to reworking their projects into one dance, they will begin to understand that change will be necessary. Their work will be manipulated and changed to benefit the dance as a whole. Once they open themselves to the many possibilities, the risk doesn't seem so unnerving. For the dance teacher, a delicate balance exists between being open to the integrity of the students' ideas about the work and a surrendering of the personal views of those in the role of director.

 **Obstacle**

Getting students to let go of the masterpiece

 **Solutions**

- Leading the way, I try to include the class in the role of director. We begin by observing the movements of the small projects to determine which groups could work as complements or as contrasts. I may choose two groups to dance simultaneously but separated in the space. While they dance, I imagine the possibilities of blending the movement through choreographic techniques. For example, if the groups are moving forward and backward, I may suggest that the groups cross each other. Or if the groups are in circles moving together and apart, I may suggest the circles cross or weave to show a relationship between the groups. Another idea would be for one group to work in a very large circle while the other group works in a smaller circle within the large one. After demonstrating an idea or several ideas that will possibly work, many students get excited when they see how two simple dances could look entirely different through group relationships.

- In a dance work with a class of advanced third graders, students decided to divide their dance projects into four 8-beat phrases. The phrases were shuffled together and inserted throughout the dance as a whole. The students also repeated some of the phrases, changed the direction of the movement, and moved in juxtaposition. The dance required great focus in order to start on cue. By the time the choreography was finished, the phrases appeared as responses to other group movements. It was a dance of relationships.

- There are many choreographic ideas for incorporating dance projects into one dance, such as repetition (repeating phrases), pauses, energy contrasts (smooth versus sharp; gentle versus strong), canon (like rounds in music), call and response, mirroring, overlaying movement, and delayed starts (for example, movement begins 4 or 8 beats apart). For further ideas, there are many books written on choreographic techniques and how to use the methods to build dances.

 Tip

Be aware of the students' abilities: What are they able to do? How able are they to focus on movement, sequence, and cues? What is the level of their commitment to dance? What is the level of their commitment to performance? There is a thin line between challenging students and defeating their spirit. Be aware!

 Trench Truth

When I received the information for the daCi (dance and the Child international) conference, I read it to my third-grade students. I wanted to understand how they viewed dance and themselves as dancers. I also wanted to inspire them to greater challenges. I explained that the conference was in Canada and that children from around the world would attend. They would be in fifth grade for the conference date. The students were thrilled. They started talking about a dance they could create, costuming, music, and the number of students who could go. They wanted to know whether they would fly, and a boy suggested that his dad could drive because he worked for a bus company. They wanted to know whether they would camp or sleep in a hotel. The discussion escalated into a frenzy of excitement. Finally, one boy said,

"If we're going to Canada, we'd better get dancing because we have a lot to learn."

It would be great to offer them the opportunity to perform internationally. But the wonderful moment was to have them consider it and feel competent to perform in such a large event. Dance had touched their lives.

Rehearsing

When the dances are ready to be performed and the students are aware of the performance rules (see appendix A), we proceed with the rehearsals and performances. Rehearsal is an intense practice during which details are ironed out. The students need to understand and perform every aspect of the dance from the introduction to entering the dance space to taking the bow and exiting. In rehearsal, I have the students concentrate on focus, movement cues, smooth transitions, and the performance rules that are discussed in appendix A. Nothing new will be added or changed at this point unless adjustments are needed for students who will be absent.

 **Obstacle**

Getting the students to rehearse

 **Solutions**

- After the reworking stage, the rehearsal for performance begins. During the dance class, my students rehearse the entire dance about three to six times. At this level of dance, it appears that I am asking a lot of them. Many times the students groan as they tire of the repetition. My response is, "Why do you groan? You should be thanking me for giving you the time to practice. I want you to look good and be proud of your work." Then, it becomes a joke. So when I say, "Let's try it one more time from the beginning," the class responds, "Thank you, Dr. Dance, for letting us practice."

- In the informal or grade-level performance, the students practice their dances during class. There is no major rehearsal for the performance.

- Throughout the creative process, I introduce and enforce the performance rules. When the students get to the rehearsal and performance stages, they know what to anticipate and how to handle the unexpected, and many of their fears are manageable.

 Tip

A rehearsal should be intense as far as the details and logistics are concerned, but the atmosphere should build a sense of accomplishment and pride. Yelling about every detail or mistake beats the children down. They have already worked hard and should be ready for the payoff.

 **Trench Truth**

My dear friend Audrey Jung from Virginia Commonwealth University visited my students during the last week of school. Three classes performed for her. Curious about their process, she questioned them at length. Although I could hear many of my own little phrases and motivating statements coming from them, I was quite proud of their intelligent and heartfelt responses. "What do you like about dance?" she asked. Some said they liked creating, making up their own movements, and trying new ideas. They were excited about the different ways they could dance a particular idea, and they commented on how they tried to create things differently each time. They told her, "You don't have to do the same old, same old. Try new things." These were phrases that I had repeated to them many times.

They explained that they liked working together because they got to know each other differently. One example was that Johnny didn't like Billy, but after creating a dance together, they became friends. In a passionate way, they expressed that each person has something to say, and that they thought that they could help each other by listening.

The most profound statement from young children was that they liked practicing. They realized that the more they practiced, the better they became. It was a sense of mastery.

And, of course, they liked dance because they received applause. I rarely give the students any gifts or tangible prizes, because I want them to learn that intrinsic rewards are of great importance.

Audrey's visit provided many wonderful moments of realizing that these young children understood and had experienced dance and the creative process. As she left she said, "There's something magical about that group of students." How well I knew it!

Rehearsing for a Formal Performance

A rehearsal for a formal performance includes all students and teachers who are involved in the show. They practice a procession into the space; sequence dances and music; determine the placement of musical instruments; practice speaking in front of an audience (if they are speaking); set stage lighting; and gather the actual visuals such as props, costumes, and artwork.

 Obstacle

Knowing how many and what type of rehearsals to have

 **Solutions**

- The day before the program the students and teachers who are involved meet for a rehearsal. The cast varies from 60 to 100 students. The whole program is put together from the entrance to the final bows. This rehearsal is the first time that the entire cast sings together and observes the other dances. It usually goes quite well because all the students want to do their best to impress their peers. It takes about 2 hours to piece together a 45-minute program. Usually there is a 15-minute recess in the middle of the rehearsal.

- Many students are unaware of time in relationship to the performance. They become aware that there will soon be an audience. Although they have been told for several weeks about the performance, the fact that the performance is tomorrow is a new awareness.

- As we go through each step of the program, I explain the details and we practice them, and I answer questions.

- On the day of the performance the students perform a dress rehearsal for the entire school. The kids in the audience sit on the floor and there are chairs for the faculty and other visitors. By this point in time, the kinks have been worked out (we hope): entrance, order, performance rules, rolling the piano on and off, taped music, lighting, costumes, the awareness of the audience, giving out and collecting the props, and the classroom teachers' role in assistance with transition and discipline. The dress rehearsal is usually 50 to 55 minutes long, because we may pause to remind the students of a detail that may have escaped.

- The dress rehearsal is the time for the students to focus without giving in to the distraction of an audience.

 **Tip**

Estimate a generous amount of time for rehearsals. When there is time to work out the logistics of the performance, the sense of urgency is dismissed and more is accomplished in a shorter time.

Trench Truth

If organized well, the rehearsal can be extremely productive. For the most part, the students will be cooperative, especially if they realize that there will be an audience in 24 hours. I prefer a rehearsal that is relatively low key—so a calmness exists. There is no need to yell at or discipline the children. The group can focus on the logistics of the event.

Rehearsing in the Space

For young students it is best to rehearse in the space where the performance will take place. Most students do not create or practice their dances with the audience in mind. When the dance space is changed, they are totally disoriented.

 **Obstacle**

Using a small or different space

 **Solutions**

- I usually have students practice their dances in the performance space, which saves time during rehearsal. If a program is performed at a different location, I have the floor taped similar to the markings on the floor in the gym. The visual cues such as lines or dots assure the students of a similarity in performance space.

- If the gym is small, as it is in my school, students must rehearse transitions. Everyone needs to understand the order of the program. Time and patience are required to work out transitions between speaking parts, songs, and dances.

- When combining dance and music in the same program, you need to creatively work out space problems. The school music teacher usually has all the students sing together, producing a full sound of voices and musical rhythm instruments. The students are in four rows with the first row sitting, the second sitting on their heels, the third kneeling up, and the fourth standing. On occasion, we have used risers for primary grades, but they take up a lot of the space that elementary students need when they dance.

- The performance space is similar to a thrust stage. The students are across the back of the stage for music and use the thrust for dance. Because there are no exits or wings in which to stand, the students rotate in the space. I divide them in half, and they walk to the far ends of the gym while the dancers take their places.

- The order of the program requires organization. The students may sing, followed by dancing, a speaking part, then singing again. The order varies according to the development of the theme. The sequence is important because the point is to keep mass movement to a minimum. The entire cast must move quickly and quietly to the next part of the show. Transitions are usually 10 to 15 seconds.

- There are speaking parts to introduce the songs or dances. These usually focus on the history, science, or story line of the program. We have auditions for speaking parts. Before the rehearsal, the selected speakers have practiced speaking clearly and slowly with a microphone. They also need to know their order in the program and how to make their transition to speak.

 Tip

Draw a picture of an audience on a large piece of cardboard. Let your students practice and rehearse in relationship to it; it will give them a sense of orientation.

 **Trench Truth**

When choosing speaking parts, I refrain from asking the classroom teacher or the class who the best readers are. The best readers are not the best presenters. The criteria are that the student have a strong, clear voice; can enunciate; and is able to read with expression. To help the students phrase properly, I usually mark the readings with one blue line for every pause and two red lines for every stop. After I choose the speakers, there is a rehearsal reading. We begin with all of the speakers reading at the same time. This teaches them to think about what they are saying. For clarity, they practice reading with exaggerated lip movement. The more exaggeration there is in rehearsal, the clearer their delivery in performance. Finally, the students practice individually speaking into the microphone. The speakers will also need to know when they will speak in the program and the logistics of when and how to move to the microphone.

Dressing Up the Gym

This is the time when I try to delegate authority to the art teacher, classroom teacher, parents, or friends. If I am involved with the performance, setting up scenery or other decorations becomes very time consuming. It is important to ask for help.

 **Obstacle**

Decorating the gym

 Solutions

- A small stage lighting system is available, which consists of 12 8-inch Fresnels, some cables, and a small dimmer control system. Lighting equipment is set up in the gym for third- through fifth-grade students. Although not an elaborate setup, it gives the students an experience similar to one in a theater. I tell the students that the lighting is a gift from me in appreciation for their hard work on the performance. It is a gift because lighting equipment is not set up for every performance.
- Artwork and scenery are created during the visual arts classes.

 **Tip**

Estimate a generous amount of time for building or decorating the set.

Trench Truth

My friends are still laughing at my incredible lack of understanding time. One year the children were performing *The Yellow Submarine*. I asked my friends for help with the props and told them it would take about 3 to 4 hours. I wanted a rolling submarine large enough for 10 children to stand inside. It needed a little hatch or back door from which the children would exit. We started working, and we worked and worked and worked. Four weekends later it was finished. It was a great submarine, but the amount of time we spent on it was far from my creative comprehension.

Preparing Psychologically

Paralleling the strong emphasis of performance is the psychological preparation for the dance event. A positive performance experience is top priority. Knowledge of what to expect, how to present, how to make adjustments while performing, and the feelings that can be anticipated is part of the training for performance. Setting the scene and preparing the students for this experience are huge responsibilities. The experience of performance could have a lasting impact on each dancer. The fragile egos of elementary students need to be gently guided through the experience.

I have seen merciless dance performances where children have fallen, forgotten what to do, or stood on stage crying while the audience screamed with laughter. What a humiliating and confusing experience for the child! Adults may think that it's cute, but these experiences will never be forgotten and may prevent the child from ever performing again.

 **Obstacle**

Preparing the psyche for the dance performance

 **Solutions**

- I have been fortunate to have the opportunity to work with the same students for many years. The process of learning to perform has been slowly nurtured, and I have had time to learn when and how to encourage each student to go further. Together, we have seen and experienced many dance performances. The students are offered performance venues of informal showings at each grade level and an integrated program performed for parents. Other opportunities for performance vary each year. Every formal and informal performance is videotaped and viewed by each class as an instructional lesson. From these previous experiences, we have been able to refer to and discuss problems, make adjustments, and develop guidelines for creating and performing.
- I have never had a child of any age (3 and up) cry during a performance. There have been many who have fallen or lost their hats or shoes, but they were prepared to continue. The performance rules

(see appendix A) are part of my everyday lessons. The rules become implanted in their minds, and they know what is expected of them and what they can expect. Through this method, they enter the performance with confidence that they can handle the situation.

Tip

Take the time to psychologically prepare your students for performance. They will gain confidence in being in public, and it will be with them for the rest of their lives.

Trench Truth

Several years into the program, I was assigned to a high-risk school that had had a new dance teacher every year. The children were from extremely troubled home situations and demonstrated many problems at school. I started the school year with a positive attitude toward my new challenge. However, by the middle of the year, I felt that I had spent my time harnessing the energies of my fifth-grade students and trying to teach them the basic concepts of movement.

When I thought that they could work with each other, I suggested that we have a performance for all fifth-grade classes. They just stared at me, and then each class expressed that they would be embarrassed and didn't want others to laugh at them. The following week, I told each class that the other fifth graders were interested in performing and that they could also have the experience (a little motivational fib). At the time I don't think I realized what I was in for: There were several absences in each class every week. There were also student withdrawals and new students to bring on board weekly. Although the students chose their teams, they argued, cried, quit, and pouted throughout the process. I expended a great deal of energy helping them solve problems and motivating them to continue. I kept them on task by allowing short work periods and brief showings of what they had accomplished. Fortunately, two or three groups in each class focused and began to come up with some clever ideas. This created a healthy competition that motivated everyone. I hyped them up with an upbeat tone and positive reinforcement.

On the day of the informal showing, they entered the gym in a fearful silence. The teachers and principal were present. Several minutes later, Annie, an extremely disturbed child, came running in along with the school counselor. Annie had been in a hospital for mental illness the week before and had thrown temper tantrums that morning in the class. She had been crying with the counselor when she realized that it was time for the dance showing. She said, "I need to go to my performance because my team needs me and we have been working on this for weeks." She joined the class as if everything were normal. All the classes performed with confidence as if they were professionals, and the audience cheered them on.

After the performance, each adult gave their praises and commented on what really impressed them. Then I told the students how proud I was of them and said, "Is there anyone who would like to perform this afternoon for the third and fourth grades?" Every hand went up instantly. The dance showing was truly a success story and a motivating opportunity for all involved. And as for Annie, I realized that through the dance process she had found a sense of commitment and pride in her accomplishments.

Informal Grade-Level Program

The informal grade-level program is an introduction to performance for all students, especially for those who are new to the school. Although most students are involved in other types of performance such as singing, performing class plays, and giving book reports, dance brings its unique feelings and experiences. It is an opening of self through the instrument of the body. There is no place to hide. Each student is out there! The informal showing is the practice session for getting used to presenting themselves and their bodies; getting used to the feelings of fear, embarrassment, pride, or whatever they may experience; and getting used to the formality wrapped in the joy of movement.

Other than the classroom teachers, the informal performance is reserved for those who experienced the creative process. Judgment is reserved for those who have been through the process. When the audience includes parents or other classes that have not experienced the process, the focus changes. If parents are present the student's focus is not on the group or class but on "me and my relationship to my parents." For the informal showing, my goal is for the focus to be on the process.

 **Obstacle**

Setting up an informal performance

 **Solutions**

- The students perform one or two informal performances a year. It may include three or four classes from one grade level, or in schools with smaller enrollments, a few classes that are close in age range.
- The grade-level performance is structured. The students sit in their assigned places, usually in the form of a theater-in-the-round. As each class is introduced, the dancers quietly take their places. When all are silent and still, the music or beginning cue is given and the dancers perform. A bow is choreographed in the dance, and the dancers pause for their applause. The dancers return to their seating places and the other classes perform. Because this is an informal showing, the situation is used as a teaching opportunity

that may include instructions or comments that would not have been given during a formal performance.

- In the grade-level performance, the concepts or dance elements from which the dances are created are usually the same. An interesting aspect is how the material is developed, organized, dressed, and staged differently by each class. The music is chosen during the creative process and reflects the personality of the dance.

- As a class or as groups within the class, the students decide what they will wear. The costuming is simple and based on color. A costume is something that everyone in the group owns, such as blue T-shirts and blue jeans or white shorts and red shirts.

- How a dance is staged depends on the ability of the class. Staging could be as simple as each group walking out to the performance space and performing their dance, and it could escalate to a group ensemble of unison movement followed by small group works interacting.

- At the end of the showing, I invite the audience to give feedback. Several students and teachers compliment the dancers. I encourage the students to use phrases such as "I like the way the students in Mrs. Smith's class did . . . ," or "I thought it was very interesting the way everyone did . . . ," or "There was a particular group in Mrs. Brown's class that did . . . ." My purpose behind this type of critique is to keep the experience positive and not to permit the students to single out friends. Yes, there are many very good dancers in each class who are certainly noticed and receive acknowledgment. But my goal is to build team spirit or oneness as a performing group.

- During the informal showing I have occasionally had students respond that certain classes always get the good music or the good dances. I only state that the comment is inappropriate at that time, but it will be discussed later. Later during the dance class, the comment is discussed and the students come to the realization that they get out of the dance what they put into it. It is a painful realization, but a stepping-stone for growth.

- The experience of an informal showing is intense but rewarding for the students. The intensity comes from performing and showing their work to their peers. They strive to perform their dances smoothly without mistakes. And, in most cases, they unite as a class with the stronger students signaling and supporting the weaker or the more distracted ones.

- I try to get the classroom teachers to attend the performance, because it provides them with another perspective of each of their students' development. Although each class works from the same criteria, interpretations are very different and are always recognized by the teachers. Most teachers are amazed at the students who shine and assume leadership roles. These are not always the best readers or the most knowledgeable in the classroom. The teachers always give feedback on the students' ability to work cooperatively, which acknowledges how the students have included the children who never get along in class or on the playground.

Tip

In every performing situation, allow the students to learn about presenting themselves to the audience. Implement the performance rules (see appendix A).

Trench Truth

The details of an informal showing needs to be explained to all involved. The first year that I was in a particular school, the schedule was set up so that I saw a different group of third graders every day. Because it was their first informal showing, I wanted it to be a learning experience on a very small scale. I told the students that the audience would only be the third graders and teachers. When I scheduled the informal showing, the teachers rearranged their schedules to accommodate it. What I didn't realize was that they were so excited that they invited parents, grandparents, and friends to the showing. Much to my surprise, when the students walked in for their small-scale, informal showing, so did about 35 guests.

This experience made me realize I need to be clear with the teachers and principal about my goals, intentions, and invitations. I am now aware that in some schools the thinking is that if a few classes gather for a performance, then it is automatically a school assembly—everyone shows up!

Preparing for the Formal Performance

Performance is presenting the best that each student is able to offer at a given time. It offers a sense of accomplishment, an intangible reward. Feelings of pride, self-worth, and confidence grow as students learn a life skill of presenting themselves in public. When the students create ideas and movements, they assume ownership of the work and express personal pride. Performance channels efforts of total focus and personal control. It climaxes in applause as an audience becomes involved. In the performance setting, students begin to experience a giving and receiving relationship with the audience.

The formal program is an integration of the arts (dance, music, and visual arts) with other areas of the curricula. This annual event is offered to every grade level. In schools with a small population, there may be only two programs: primary grades and elementary grades.

 **Obstacle**

Setting up an integrated curricula performance

 **Solutions**

- Arts and classroom teachers meet to brainstorm for possible program themes based on the curriculum that will be developed in the classroom or other areas of interest. It may take several meetings to reach an agreement on a theme or on a different approach for a program. A great amount of thought and discussion on the pros and cons of every idea is considered. When a theme is decided, everyone is expected to contribute to the program. Finding a meeting of the minds on how and what needs to be introduced to the students can be very difficult.

- If the arts are integrated with the classroom curriculum, the role of the classroom teacher is to develop the concepts on which the program will be based, such as history, science, or literature. The classroom teacher is expected to encourage the students to assume responsibility through research and other projects. Many teachers enjoy working with the students on choral reading and on speaking parts that explain the theme or serve as narration for dance or music. Working with the information and research from the students, the arts teachers collaborate on their approach for the program. Music, song, and dance support different aspects of the theme. In the visual arts class, students create props, costumes, and scenery for the performance. For example, for a rain forest theme, the students created scenery that looked like a rain forest: trees, bushes, leaves hanging from a canopy effect, and painted backdrops of forest scenes. They constructed animal hats and tails that served as their costumes for dance. Of course, this is the ideal, and I must admit that I have been fortunate to enjoy the ideal on many occasions.

- There have also been occurrences when the classroom teachers did not want to be part of the arts performance. They may think that arts programs should be the project of the arts teachers. Other teachers agree to the ideas but do not follow through with commitment. Unfortunately, when the concepts are not taught in the classroom, the groundwork ends up as the role of the arts teachers. If this is the case, it may take two or three classes before the process of creating art is able to begin. It has been my experience that many classroom teachers who do not follow through really are unaware of what to do. Performance and the process of creativity are out of their realm. These teachers are generally happy to cooperate if they are given specific instructions. So I have learned to be a little more aggressive during meetings. I may state exactly what the children will need to know to build a dance on a theme.

- When the groundwork is laid, the students discuss the theme and brainstorm for ideas to create a dance. The creative process begins and concludes six to eight weeks later in a formal performance for their family and friends. During this time, there are many faculty meetings for discussing the progress and coordinating ideas. The program is a major undertaking, and everyone is vital to its success.
- Costuming is kept simple with emphasis on color: for example, a red, orange, yellow, or blue shirt to symbolize the students' roles. The students usually wear dark pants or blue jeans and tennis shoes. Wings, hats, and other props are created in the visual arts classes, and the students rarely purchase costumes or costume material.

 Tip

The greater your communication with the classroom teachers, the easier the process of planning the performance will be.

 **Trench Truth**

I have worked in several schools where a particular performance theme was traditional. The script, songs, and dances were exactly the same year after year. Not realizing the magnitude of this situation, I quickly said that I would help with the dances. The teachers in turn gave me the music and written-down movements. I asked whether it was all right to expand the dances. Most agreed and said that they would rehearse in their classes. After three classes, I realized that the class rehearsals were not based on what we created in dance. When I addressed this concern with the teachers, they dismissed me from the work, saying that they knew the movement they wanted and would finish the work in their classrooms. Clear communication was obviously lacking.

Directing Formal Performances

With respect to all involved, one person needs to be the director. I decide early in the process who it will be, and I let that person be responsible. If not, all teachers have a tendency to take over and it becomes a state of chaos. Each adult involved needs to know specifically what his role is in the performance.

 **Obstacle**

Directing the formal performance

 **Solutions**

- The night of the performance the students meet their classroom teachers in the cafeteria or a large room. Parents hurry to find a seat because 98 percent of the students and their parents are present. The audience sits in a large semicircle several rows deep; space is tight. Parents take pictures and video recordings of the entire program. The lighting of the program produces a magical spell on the audience—they respond accordingly, as if they are in a theater and not at a ball game in a gym. However, there have been times when parents yelled out something like, "Go, Johnny!" and after the dance or song I interjected a comment on audience expectations such as, "Audience, please respect the performers and give them quiet," or "Audience, please do not distract the performers."

- The teachers sit on the side nearest the students, the music teacher sits by the piano, and I stand at the dimmer control system of the lighting system in the back center of the audience. There are few signals during the program. I may click the clave for a dance signal, and the music teacher may signal to rise or move. The program moves quickly and smoothly, most of the time. The performance is usually 30 to 45 minutes long.

- The program begins as the students form a procession into the performance space. It is up to them now! Nurtured along the creative path, they earned a gift, which is now theirs to enjoy. The end result is truly gratifying. They assume responsibility and perform with joy and commitment. The parents are filled with pride and begin to understand how the arts and the other curricula connect.

As I remember the crying, the arguing, the creating, the growing, I know that this process has affected the students' lives.

- The program ends with a group bow and a presentation of flowers to the arts teachers. I always teach the students to present flowers (even if they are wildflowers or artificial flowers). This gesture teaches the students that they have received the gift of performance, and they need to say, "Thank you for the experience."

 Tip

Take time to enjoy the applause—you deserve it!

 **Trench Truth**

Danny was a shy boy who was in the dance program in kindergarten, first grade, and a transition first and second grade. The last year he attended the school his class performed *The Rain Forest*, an integrated curricula program. The program was held at the end of May. I saw Danny once after the performance, when the students viewed the videotape of the program and talked about the experience.

The next school year, he entered second grade in another school. In October, his new school counselor, who is a personal friend, contacted me to say that Danny had been referred to her because he had not made friends and appeared depressed. In the course of their many meetings, Danny told her that he had attended Sacajawea Elementary School. She asked him who had been his dance teacher. He responded, "Dr. Dance . . . And last year we put on a program about the rain forest . . . and I was a Blue Frog . . . they're the poisonous ones . . . and my mom came to see me dance . . ." and he talked on and on. His performance was the door through which he could communicate. The counselor was so pleased because she said it was the first time he had smiled during the school year. Dance had opened the door of communication for Danny; it had touched his life.

Reviewing the Process

The dance class following the performance is a meeting time in which to review the experience of the creative process. Although the students have become a team, each has had different experiences, memories, and outcomes.

 **Obstacle**

Being open about the process

 **Solutions**

- During the review, the students share the comments of their parents and relatives who attended the performance. Or in the case of an informal showing, they discuss the comments that were given at the end of the showing.

- During the sharing I encourage the students to really think of the comments and not say, "They thought it was good." When they give me this response, I tell the students:

  > Ask questions, such as "What was good about it? What did you like? What did you think of the part where . . . ? what did you think about the music?" the next time someone tells you that it was good. When you ask questions, it gives you feedback as to what worked for the audience, what the strengths of the program were, and what needed improvement.

- The students observe the videotape of their dance two or three times. The students enjoy seeing themselves and are able to enjoy the finished product. During the first viewing of the work, the students usually laugh at themselves, at some unexpected thing that may have happened, or at the response of the audience. The second viewing is to examine and discuss the work. The third viewing is in light of the comments that were discussed.

- After we discuss and enjoy the surface information, we seriously discuss the emotional aspects of the process. Students share what they learned from the experience. Some students share their innermost feelings while others brush off the whole experience. I usually try to sum up my experience: where I felt we had gone, the boulders blocking our progress, the solving of problems, the joy of their performance, and the growth that was evident.

Tip

Reflection is essential because it shows us where we have traveled and where we have arrived. Make time for this stage of the process.

Trench Truth

A review of the process is usually ongoing. I have learned much about my students and myself throughout every aspect of the process. For example, Mrs. Einstein's class of intellectually gifted and challenged students completed small-group projects. After I observed their wonderful projects, I envisioned the parts coming together, creating a modern dance work of contrasts. In the reworking process, I made suggestions such as, "How would it look if this group started and that group delayed their start by 8 beats?" They tried the first suggestion but were half-hearted. My second suggestion was to have two groups dance simultaneously. I felt the class totally shut down. I ended the class by saying that my ideas were just suggestions, and I wanted them to think about different ways to bring the dance together as a whole. The following week, I found a letter in my mailbox:

DR. DANCE

I THINK YOU SHOULD LET US DO OUR DANCES MORE ON OUR OWN. IT RUINS OUR CREATIVITY WHEN YOU TAKE OVER OUR DANCES! IT'S NICE THAT YOU TRY TO HELP US AND I KNOW IT'S YOUR JOB. BUT YOU HELP US TOO MUCH! I'M SERIOUS ABOUT THIS! PLEASE TRY TO DO SOME THING ABOUT IT!

SINCERELY,

ANOMYMUS

It was a great letter that opened the door for discussing the process. After reading the letter, I announced to the class that I had received it and that I wasn't upset or angry about it. I wished, however, that the person who wrote it had discussed the concern with me. My comments diverted from the letter, and I used the following analogy of baking a cake to express my views:

Your dances have great ingredients, but if you put the eggs and milk in one bowl, the flour in another, and leave the sugar, chocolate bits, vanilla, and butter on the counter, you will only have ingredients. If you blend them together, bake for 30 minutes, and then frost, you will have a scrumptious cake. That's what I was trying to do with your dance.

The students responded that I was too enthusiastic. I asked too much from them, and I overwhelmed them. They really liked what they had created and didn't want to change anything, because the dances were their own ideas. Each group wanted to be unique and not a part of a whole dance. They wanted their part to be shown and noticed. Individual recognition was their goal. Realizing where they were in their process, I agreed and we worked together on transitions from one small group to another.

After the informal grade-level performance, we watched the videotape and discussed the process. They saw their work in relation to the other classes and knew that their small group work was good. But they were amazed at the dance of Mrs. Franklin's class, who were also intellectually gifted and challenged. Mrs. Franklin's class had taken the challenge that I offered them. Not only did the students use my suggestions, but they also understood the process and came up with their own ideas to complement and contrast movement. The movement belonged to the class, and there was no acknowledgment of any individual who created it.

Mrs. Einstein's class wanted to know how Mrs. Franklin's class created their dance. I explained that Mrs. Franklin's class took the risk to create something new with their dance projects. They combined them, and they used delayed starts and canon form. It was a bit confusing and frustrating for them at times. But one of the reasons that it worked was that everyone was willing to let go of their creations and take the ideas down a new street.

Some of Mrs. Einstein's students were angry that they didn't get the "good dance." I explained that I offered them the challenge, but they were not ready to risk letting go of their own projects. They appeared to understand and now had a reference for where dance could lead when they accepted changes. One girl summed up the situation, "Now I understand about making the cake. All of our ingredients were on the kitchen counter."

Dance Education for Parents and Faculty

Putting Creative Dance in the Spotlight

The success of an arts program in a school or school district is dependent on the value placed on the program by the administration, the faculty, and the parents. Music and visual arts programs have been featured in public education for decades. Dance education, however, is relatively new on the scene and brings with it a wide range of opinions and views about the definition of dance.

 **Obstacle**

Educating the community about dance

 **Solutions**

- I began by acknowledging the views of the community regarding dance. Some people viewed dance strictly as social dance or shaking the body—bump and grind. Chorus lines and Broadway dance entered the minds of many. Others thought of dance as an activity for girls and people with inadequate athletic ability. Still others viewed dance class as a time for fun, not for education. Dance also stirred up fears in adults about their own movement ability and how they may have been embarrassed about dance during their lives. These parents were eager to excuse their children from the dance opportunity. Most were unaware of the creative process and of the benefits experienced by the class as a whole and as individuals.

- Dance has many different styles and milieus. In each community the purpose and desired outcome of dance education must be determined and weighed. Sometimes, I have surprised myself about the reasons and courses of action that I have taken to promote dance and the understanding of dance. Impressing the public is not my ultimate goal, but I am very much aware that the taxpayers are supporting the dance program in the public school setting. Keeping dance in the public eye, therefore, is integral to the continuation of the program.

- Dance is a performing art, and performance is a major emphasis of the program. Through a variety of performance-oriented activities, I offer the public a view of dance. In the schools where I teach, each grade level has one integrated curricula program every year. In addition, students may be asked to perform dance for parent luncheons and teas, lecture-demonstrations, Parent Teacher Association (PTA) meetings, or parent–student classes. My intention is for the parents and the general public not only to see the children in a dance setting, but also to help parents and the public understand the process and the benefits that the arts offer to their children.

 Tip

Seize every opportunity to publicly present creative dance.

 Trench Truth

During the first year of the program, the president of the PTA was eager to increase the number of parents in attendance for the PTA's January meeting. She requested a dance presentation of third through fifth graders, which she hoped would bring the parents to the meeting and serve as a stepping-stone for understanding the creative dance program. Fifty students volunteered for a lecture-demonstration program.

With the students having a limited knowledge of dance, the lecture-demonstration began with an explanation of the goals of the program and the role of creativity in self-expression. Drawing on a variety of ways to present the dance elements, the third graders demonstrated level changes, nonlocomotors, and shapes (angle, curve, straight, and twist). With an emphasis on contrasts, the fourth graders demonstrated tempo, shapes, and level changes moving through space. The fifth graders performed small-group choreographic studies (set movements based on certain dance elements) that included moving together and apart and the previously mentioned elements. The 10 small groups staggered their entrances by 8 counts and repeated their studies, which expanded the work and juxtaposed the movements. Although level changes through space at a slow tempo held the attention of the audience, the parents and teachers responded enthusiastically when they viewed shapes in the air and quick staccato changes in level and shape. The choreographic studies appeared to be somewhat familiar and comfortable to the audience.

Most elementary level teachers were present and appeared to watch their students with great pride. At the end of the evening, their remarks addressed the ability of the students to work cooperatively and with care for each other. As the parents were leaving, many remarked that they had never seen creative dance. Several parents commented on the uninhibited movement of the boys and on the ability of the students to focus. A few of the fathers mentioned the students' ability to work with concepts that were somewhat abstract. A couple of mothers commented that if they had known that their children were going to roll on the floor, they would have dressed them in old clothes. Parents and teachers remarked that the demonstration did not resemble any recognizable dance forms, but they were pleased with the enthusiasm of the students to move creatively and express themselves publicly.

Educating Parents

Early in developing the creative dance program, the students were involved in a lecture-demonstration for the parents. Since that time, the parents had many opportunities to observe and experience creative dance. One of the most beneficial ways of educating the parents in the creative dance process was to involve them in parent–student dance classes.

 **Obstacle**

Providing opportunities for parents to be involved in the creative dance process

 **Solutions**

- A 1-hour creative dance class for each grade level was held in the evenings for students, parents, and teachers. This wasn't a set program—it was quite flexible regarding the needs of the school year and the students. Usually 10 to 30 parents attended with their children.

- The parent–student class was designed to emphasize the creative process through small-group work. We began with personal introductions and a brief discussion of creative dance. Afterward, we performed a warm-up, usually followed by progressions (a movement or a series of movements across the room) that focused on the dance elements that would be used in the choreographic studies that evening. For example, knowledge of 8 beats of music was required in the choreography. The dance progression was built on movement that changes every 8 counts. For example, move forward for 8 beats, move in a circular pathway for 8 beats, move in place for 8 beats, and freeze for 8 beats.

- The class was then divided into small groups of five to six members. I said a few words about the need for cooperation and collaboration. A demonstration of the requirements for the choreographic study was given. The requirements varied for each class and were limited to musical beats. The groups had 15 to 20 minutes to complete the choreography and to practice for showing their work.

- Each group performed the dance work, which was analyzed for requirements and discussed for interpretation by the other class members. After the performance, the class discussed the creative process and their feelings about working in a group. Usually, the parents were amazed about the differences in interpretation of requirements, the group process, and the joy of performance. For me, the joy was in watching the parents interacting with their children and learning to move freely again.

- Parents voiced an eagerness to become more knowledgeable and to continue participation in the creative dance process. They witnessed dance as an expression and an exploration of other areas of the curricula. They also acknowledged the positive results in their children.

 Tip

The parent–student class is a great method of helping parents to get on board. Organize one in your school.

 Trench Truth

The process of creating dance in a parent–student setting was an eye-opener. Most of the parents entered the space with serious and silent faces. I realized that they feared the unknown of the dance class. Most made it through the warm-up and progressions, but it was the interaction of group work where it was really fascinating. There were children who took over or had temper tantrums when the parents wouldn't perform their ideas. These were children who would have never responded in that manner in the classroom. There were adults who stuck their heels in the ground and didn't want to cooperate with others. There were families in which the father took complete control of the situation and didn't allow the other group members to express their ideas. There were groups who couldn't think of any ideas. There were parents who thought they knew best, and although there was much conflict in the groups, they wanted to do the organizing. There were groups where fathers were full of play and encouraged everyone in the group to create and move with great energy. Each individual struggled to find her role in the group, and while doing so, movement ideas were being generated. During the process, unique and interesting movement was created, rehearsed and performed. Through the performance aspect, the team united and there was a feeling of accomplishment. As the families left the class, I noticed discussion and excitement in their faces as they shared their experiences. For a moment in time, their lives were changed.

If You Don't Have the Principal's Support, Don't Take the Job

The role of the school principal is crucial to the strength of the arts program. When the administration views the arts as a privilege for the students, the experience of teaching is sweet and rewarding. The students focus on the class; discipline is not a major issue; the curricula begin to connect; the students' work is honored; teachers respond enthusiastically; and the parents embrace the program. I have experienced this utopia!

 **Obstacle**

Working with the administration

 Solutions

- Many principals are lacking understanding and appreciation of the arts. In these situations, arts teachers are left to fend for themselves as an outsider within the school. The principal would prefer to support the classroom teachers rather than upset the staff with concerns of the itinerant teachers. It is essential to communicate with the principal about your goals, teamwork, and your management system. Have him come in to see a class or view a showing of work. Get the principal involved—win him over!

- One of the best ways to win over the principal is to bring positive recognition to the school. My method is through performance in all milieus. The parents become involved and share their joy and appreciation with the principal. You begin to "score points."

- I was in a situation where administrative support was swayed by the classroom teachers and not by understanding or discussion of the arts process. For example, the elementary students were assigned a written critique during a primary student performance. The classroom teachers feared and complained that the students might write negative statements about the student performers. So the principal, without discussion, confiscated the critique forms before the performance. This incident discounted my role as a teacher and the entire critique process that the students had experienced as positive. I solved this problem by asking the principal to come into a critique session after the performance. There he heard the students express higher levels of thinking and the discussion that occur in critique, and he realized that it was an important educational tool.

 Tip

Before accepting a dance or arts position, discuss and determine the philosophy of the administration and the faculty on major subjects such as the creative process, the purpose and role of the arts in that school, and views on class management. If the situation appears pliable, accept the position and begin by setting up a communication system that explains the what and why of the program and the specifics that will effect the school and its philosophy.

 Trench Truth

In a school where I taught, a new principal arrived on the scene. For several classes, I was having difficulty with a boy who refused to tie his shoes. As he moved through the space, the shoe would come off and there would be a series of bumping and falling as others would stumble over him. Or he would wait until the opportune moment to kick his shoe across the room. Although he was asked to sit out, he used his time-out to distract the class. I called the principal and explained the situation, and I assumed that we were on the same wavelength. The principal came to the gym, talked to the boy, and sent him back into the dance space in his stocking feet. That didn't solve the problem; it only taught the boy that he didn't need to meet the requirements. After class, I discussed the situation with the principal. He thought that children could wear what they wanted to class because they needed to express themselves through style. We discussed the problem from the point of view of safety—we harangued about safety concerns. Moreover, I was very concerned that the boy had learned that I had no authority in the class and that he could do whatever he wanted. When I could see that I was getting nowhere in the discussion, I decided to deal with the problem myself by sending a note to the boy's parent. I also developed a brochure describing the creative dance program, the grading policies, and the dress requirements. The brochure was sent to every parent in the school.

Understanding and Accepting Creative Dance Education

I had the pleasure and the struggle of introducing the creative dance program in two elementary schools. It was a new experience for all involved. Classroom teachers were filled with apprehension about this new dance curriculum. Although there was a previous explanation regarding creative dance, its processes and its benefits, many teachers were still expecting square and folk dance to be the core of the program. Moreover, the appearance of dance educators on the scene verified that some of the physical education teachers had been replaced, and many teachers resented that fact.

In the early stages of the program, classroom teachers peered into the gym as students were crawling and slithering through the space. With puzzled looks and eyebrows raised, they turned away. Others heard noise from the gym unlike the predictable gym sounds of cheering and screaming. As they were drawn to the noise, they viewed small groups talking, arguing, and moving chaotically through the space. With smirking faces, the teachers shook their heads and walked away. Then one day I heard the teachers talking about how much the students had enjoyed dancing in class. The teachers were pleased, and the students were thrilled because they did the Virginia Reel. Well, I knew it wasn't in the classes that I had taught that day. With a little questioning, I learned that the dance was performed in the music class. This, in and of itself, was great because movement was very much a part of the music program. But what I realized was that the teachers were thrilled because the students were performing an organized dance form that was recognizable to them.

 **Obstacle**

Helping the classroom teachers understand what is happening in the creative dance class

 **Solutions**

- My goal was teacher education with concentration on the creative dance process. I began to have more conversations with classroom teachers that explained the concepts or elements that I

was teaching and how they related to the classroom curriculum. I explained the connections of dance with the writing process, number line, directions, opposites, balance, gravity, magnetic force, centrifugal force, duration of time, addition and multiplication, positive and negative space, forces of nature, energy, and so on. We discussed partnering and small-group work and its impact on activities that the teachers were doing in the classroom. I shared my views and perceptions of various students on their behaviors and growth. I extended myself through personal contacts and made a connection between dance and the classroom.

- My lecture-demonstrations, questionnaires, informal dance showings, and formal performances included the classroom teachers and were intended not only as a showing of work, but also as an informative experience for the classroom teachers about the creative dance process.

- One blessed day about two years into the program, a teacher passed by the gym and observed a class totally absorbed in watching a small-group showing. The students were in the critiquing stage. The classroom teacher was amazed by the concentration of the class and by the fact that her presence did not alter the attention of the audience and dancers. Yes, we had arrived! Results were visible to outsiders! The word spread, and after that incident other classroom teachers began to come for the last few minutes of the class to see what the students were doing. Many commented on the changes from week to week and were eager to observe the progress.

   **Tip**

As the program grows the classroom teachers begin to understand creative dance, its process, and the potential of the program. With the support of the classroom teachers, the credibility of creative dance, and an accepting environment for the students to create, dance work blossoms. Don't underestimate your power to make this miracle happen.

Trench Truth

As part of an evaluation sent to the schools from district administration, the faculty was to describe and rank the educational programs that were most effective. We worked in six teams to discuss, analyze, and evaluate the many programs that serviced the students. When the results were in, the arts program was determined to be the most effective. The classroom teachers praised the program by offering the following comments: "It reached all of the children and provided them with experiences that could not be duplicated in the classroom." "It developed connections between the arts and between the classroom curriculum." "It provided consistent class management and expectations." "It taught the students to assess their behavior and aim for higher goals." The result of the evaluation was an honor.

Getting All Teachers on Board

The most difficult aspect of a dance and arts program is that without the classroom teachers' support the job of the arts educator can become quite complex.

 **Obstacle**

Getting understanding and support from the classroom teachers

 **Solutions**

- In many cases, the creative dance and arts programs serve as a planning period that benefits the classroom teachers. Planning time is a dream come true for the classroom teachers; but for the arts teachers it becomes an albatross. After years of the arts in the schools, some classroom teachers continued to view the arts as their planning time, as a babysitting service, and as an activity that had fun as its goal. Working from this viewpoint makes the development of a strong arts program formidable. That is why I communicate with the classroom teachers about my goals, activities, and progress. I include them in the showing of dance work and in performance situations, too.

- In some schools, every assembly, holiday party, and school activity is scheduled around arts programs so as not to deprive the classroom teachers of their preparation time. Some teachers actually compare the number of preparation minutes that each receives throughout the year and adjust the schedule for equity. This is when it pays to have the principal's respect.

- There are other classroom teachers who are very flexible yet really do not understand the arts. These teachers are usually open to change and are somewhat supportive of activities and class management.

- There are always those wonderful classroom teachers who know and love the arts. They appreciate the benefits of the program and are always eager to be involved. Please, send me more of these teachers!

- On several occasions, there have been classroom teachers who allowed their students to attend arts classes if they approved of the class, but if not, they called or sent a message to say they were too busy to attend. This taught the students that the arts had little value in relation to the classroom activities.

- In other situations, the arts classes were viewed as a time for socialization. Special education classes and their aides were included in integrated arts classes. I agree that special education students should receive arts classes and should be included in the regular education classes; but inclusion needs to be on an individual basis, and placement should be determined by when each student is ready for the experience. Again, this problem needs to be worked out with the principal.

- In some situations, classroom teachers have refused to support any decisions or class management methods that were enforced in the arts. Actually, some assumed the role of a referee between the students and the arts teachers. A strong school management plan eliminates this problem.

 Tip

Give the classroom teachers or principal a detailed explanation of the concept or process that the students are experiencing in dance class. Through your communication, the administration and the faculty will support the arts and will continue to learn about the creative process.

Trench Truth

Even though university education programs acknowledge the arts, the effects that the arts have on individuals and on society continues to be dismissed.

While team teaching an arts course for master's degree education candidates, I developed great anxiety about future classroom teachers and their support of the arts. Some students in the classes had experienced the arts and were aware of the value of the arts in education. But this was not the case for the majority of the students. In discussions, many were quiet or expressed that they were unaware of what the arts were. Some had never been to an art museum or attended a dance concert, but most had been to rock concerts. Others questioned why a museum field trip to the Dynasties of China Exhibit was of value to the class. But the most distressing comment came in response to the question "What is art?" A student responded, "The arts are something you do when you have nothing else to do." Others thought that every time a person expressed herself, it was art. They refused to accept or were unaware that there are concepts of form and structure and a creative process. The syllabus for these classes focused on history and how the arts express the time periods. After lengthy reports and projects prepared by the students, there was a slight acknowledgment that the arts made a connection to their lives and to the field of teaching.

Arts education must begin at birth, and when that is not possible, it must start as soon as children enter school. With early intervention, they will develop into adults who have a passion for the arts.

The Dance Audience

Creating Dance Audiences

During the 1980s and 1990s, the national emphasis for dance education appeared to focus on the development of dance audiences. Opposed to that thinking, my ultimate goal for dance education was to foster a society that dances. It was my opinion that any other goal appeared to shortchange the students. The building of dance audiences maintained a separation between (to use old terms) dancers and nondancers. I've always dreaded this concept, because my view is that everyone is a dancer or that everyone has the right to enjoy movement. The term "nondancer" is not in my vocabulary.

When I began teaching creative dance in the Northwest, the majority of students in the schools displayed little knowledge of dance. Their views of dance were provincial. I thought that if I could get them past the giggling and embarrassment stages, their views would be malleable. But I felt as if I were charging into a herd of stampeding buffalo.

The goal of creating a dance community appeared to be quite distant, if not impossible. I needed to offer the students a variety of backdoor approaches for establishing a solid dance foundation. And with 40-minute classes that met only once a week, I found myself adapting my previous views about dance audiences. One of the backdoor approaches that I chose was the building of a dance audience—dancers as audiences, performers as observers, educated and open to all that dance could offer. I placed emphasis on the students as a worldwide dance audience, which I hoped would pave the way for them to become members of a moving community.

Before a dancing community could be established, the groundwork was laid over a five-year trial-and-error plan. There was no ordering of events; I just flooded the students with many experiences to help create movers, thinkers, and dance audiences.

 **Obstacle**

Creating dancers as dance audiences

 **Solutions**

- Through a series of videotapes, I introduced my students to an array of dance. The focus was to spur new ideas, listen to other views, and develop understanding of different points of view. As the students were bombarded with these new experiences, they increased their awareness of dance forms and of cultural expression through dance.

- Dance is often seen outside its context, which can be quite foreign. In this scenario, the students responded by giggling, displaying boredom, and expressing negative feelings. I tried to present dance in a context of culture or a concept, which gave the students the opportunity to understand it before they judged it.

- Learning to delve into dance and its meaning or the culture it represents is necessary in order for students to become dance audiences and to respond appropriately. Over the years, the students began to recognize, accept, and identify with dance.

 Tip

Always prepare the class before you show a dance videotape. Discuss costumes, contact work, time period, or history.

 Trench Truth

When I started the video enrichment program, the students were ready to laugh at everything they saw. My preparation addressed the fact that they would be seeing new and interesting dance. It would demand that they open their minds. I also told them that when people laugh at things that are not intended to be humorous, it tends to be disrespectful and also shows that they are not educated on the subject. These comments brought about immediate positive responses.

Studying Dance As Culture

Dance usually has some form of cultural expression. Before showing dance videos or learning a dance, I introduce the children to the roots of the culture; where the dance originates; the meaning of the dance within the culture; other aspects of clothing, time period, and history; and any contact work.

 **Obstacle**

Getting students to understand dance as part of culture

 **Solutions**

- Here is an example of my first effort to bridge an understanding of dance and culture: The first dance videotape that the students viewed was integrated with a third-grade social studies unit on Native American culture. My goal was to develop their awareness and understanding of cultural differences. In an effort to expose the students to something new, I heard myself repeating the phrase, "The world would be a boring place if we were all alike!"

- Before the students danced or viewed the tape, *Finding the Circle* (American Indian Dance Theater, 1989, Produced by WNET/ Thirteen in association with Tatge/Lasseur Productions, featured on Public Broadcasting Service: "Great Performances"), they were involved in researching their personal heritage. Many students discovered that they were of Native American descent. Many students of European descent became aware of their heritage for the first time. I emphasized that each student should be aware and proud of who she is and support that pride by knowing as much as possible about her ethnicity.

- The next step was to prepare the students for what they would see and hear. Aware that the dance videotape included singing, we discussed languages and the manner in which people communicate. I stressed that the more ways a person could communicate, the smarter he is—differences in language, art, dance, or music are valid and useful forms of communication. If I had not discussed language with them, the students would have giggled and mocked the singing throughout the tape. My goal was to get them to respect Native American people.

- I was very careful when I introduced the videotape. I stress *very careful*, because the students were young and the seeds of their families' values about religion were being planted. I differentiated between sacred dance of Native Americans, which is rarely shared with outsiders, and social dance, which is seen in powwows. The students realized that if they were to see sacred dance, they should be quiet and demonstrate reverence.

- Although young children are concrete in their thinking, the arts introduced the idea of symbolism to them. Understanding the use of symbolism in Native American art and dance made a smooth transition into the realm of spirituality. When students were aware that symbols represented ideas and beliefs similar to theirs, they were not as threatened by them and began to see the symbolism in their own religions. I explained that many Native American dances are prayers and are similar to ceremonies that the students may have at their churches, halls, mosques, or synagogues.

- The questions of God, gods, heaven, and being saved arose as topics for discussion. Most children are concerned about doing the right thing and want everyone else to do what is right. Sacred dance, therefore, is a very sensitive subject. Although I explained some Native American beliefs, I emphasized that people throughout the world are not alike when it comes to language, food, clothing, customs, or religion. My emphasis has nothing to do with right and wrong; it has to do with differences.

- All of this discussion, which varied in length depending on the foundation laid by the classroom teacher, was necessary for preparing the students to be respectful when they saw Native American dance. As the students discussed symbols, elements of movement, clothing, and the purpose and meaning of the dance, their perception of dance within a culture began to grow.

 Tip

Be aware of the community in which you teach. Sometimes it is important to send information to the parents about the subject matter that you will teach. Include a list of children's books that pertain to the subject matter. These books will also educate the parents.

Trench Truth

In my early years in the Northwest, I realized that many of the classroom teachers knew that there were differences in cultures, but they were unaware that these differences needed to be understood and accepted. There were many heated discussions about the difference between religious myths and religious truths. It appeared that if a teacher had a particular religious belief (predominantly Christian where I was teaching), it had to be truth; but if it was the belief of another religion, it was considered a myth. Over the years, the discussion continued and many teachers seemed to expand their views. I imagine if their views were unchanged, they avoided the subject.

Using Videotapes of Dance Genres

Dance is the umbrella term for movement that spans more than 10,000 years of humankind. A variety of dance genres should be introduced to students in order to expand their appreciation and broaden their views.

 **Obstacle**

Developing an understanding of dance genres

 **Solutions**

- I introduced a series of videotapes as a unit on African American vernacular dance. We discussed and observed the jitterbug and the swing, which elicit liveliness, surprise, verbal response, and audience involvement through clapping and movement. Students began to see a connection between traditional African dances and many African American vernacular dances, which produce audiences who observe and participate through rhythm, feelings, and vocalizations. They were able to see that vernacular dances from jazz dance to hip-hop have been assimilated into mainstream America.

- I introduced a videotape of Donald O'Connor's classic dance *Be a Clown* from the movie *Singing in the Rain*. This performance was great for introducing my students to comedy in dance. They became aware that timing is an essential element in acting and comedic dance—the goal is to have the audience respond at a precise moment based on the timing of the dancers, the music, and the props.

- Through the years, my students have learned that different styles of dance require different styles of audiences. For example, ballet audiences, who were once the royalty of Europe, have evolved as quiet spectators. The audience observes the choreography, scenery, costumes, dance technique, and story. As a modern dance audience, my students search for uniqueness of movement, meaning, and symbolism. The students have also observed and performed cultural dance as it relates to the study of a people. Rhythm dances such as tap, flamenco, body rhythms, and gum boot dances were totally new concepts for my students, but they now accept and appreciate this dance form.

- In one school, the students congregated in the gym before the classroom doors opened. I used 20 minutes, twice a week, as dance enrichment time, where I showed video clips of many dance genres. Although all of the students in the class did not view the videotapes, the impressions of the dances were carried over to class discussions and began to influence their movement.

- The dance videotape series had an extraordinary effect on my students' awareness of dance and assisted in developing their skills as a dance audience. It helped lay the foundation for dance. It made a connection between the dance skills they were learning and the final product, which is a dance.

 Tip

Make yourself a collection of dance videotapes and have them available at your fingertips. Use them to educate about the many styles of dance.

 Trench Truth

"Get Down" occurred five years into the dance program and rewarded my efforts. It was May and I had the theater lights set up for a grade-level performance. During recess I was focusing the lights as some fifth graders came in to watch and then asked questions about the lighting. The music was on in the background, and they raised the volume. Others were moving the controls on the light board. More fifth graders entered and began moving to the music. Before long someone announced that there was a dance for fifth graders in the gym and closed the door to the other students. The word spread quickly, and more fifth-grade students entered. I helped to supervise the light board and the sound equipment. About 30 students were in the gym, "dancing the night away." For me it was a sign that the dance program was successful: The students were uninhibited; they had personalized dance; and they were really enjoying themselves. When recess ended they asked whether they could have another dance the following day. Without notification, 60 students arrived with their own musical tapes and danced for another recess period. What a thrill it was for me!

Using Live Performance to Create Thinkers

The ultimate experience for dance audiences is live performance. The students actually see, hear, and feel the movement, the breath, and the rhythm. They are able to discuss the dance with the performers and ask questions about their professional lives.

 **Obstacle**

Introducing live performance to dance audiences

 **Solutions**

- For several years, the PTA has sponsored a fifth-grade field trip to the Oregon Ballet Choreographic Showcase. Before the field trip, I prepare the students for what they might see. We discuss the choreography, scenery, lighting, audience behavior, and appropriate clothing for the ballet. I explain to my students that some of the men will not have on shirts, and they will wear tights and a dance cup; and some of the women will wear leotards, body suits, and pointe shoes. The first year I took my students to the ballet, there were students from other schools sitting upstairs throwing raw vegetables down on us. Another time, a dancer's dress top fell down to her waist. Underneath the dress she had on a flesh-colored leotard, but the audience gasped. I thought that my students were adequately prepared for these surprises and handled them wisely, especially compared to the other audience members.

- The most exciting piece of this experience is to listen to the students' overjoyed comments on the return bus trip. Usually, the boys are the most expressive about the details of the dance, such as the entrances, the partner work, and the contrast of speed and strength. Their comments include "Awesome!" "I never liked ballet before because it was so slow, but this was great." "I had never been to a theater before, and I never knew that the stage was so big." "I couldn't believe how high they could jump and how fast they could turn!"

- When parents and teachers were part of the live performance experience, it brought more value to the experience for the students.

After the performance many parents were eager to fund more trips to live performances or explore the possibility of bringing local groups to the school to perform.

 Tip

Check into your state's artist-in-residence, Run for the Arts, and other programs that provide matching funds for workshops and performances.

 Trench Truth

Three years into the program, my school sponsored a modern dance performance by Kim Arrow and Rhea Slichter from Swarthmore, Pennsylvania. Students from second through fifth grades attended. The company performed three dance works: *The Mannequin,* a story about a Jewish man who struggles to maintain his person and dignity during the Nazi regime; *The Wolf,* a crafty dance expressing how nature is endangered by man; and *The Whales,* a comical dance of love. The concert was quite deep for elementary school children, and it was the first time that the students were challenged to delve into the meaning expressed through dance. The students watched the concert in silence; afterward, they questioned, discussed, compared, and contrasted meaning. They discussed Hitler, concentration camps, the Jews in hiding, and their desire to protect the wolves. They were delighted by the use of props and comedy in the whale dance. It was their first live concert, and it was extremely successful. The performance offered them the energy of live dance and revealed to some extent what dance could offer. I noticed an immediate effect on their creative dance works, and the effect was an inspiration for several years to follow.

Audience Skills

My goal for my students is to develop audience skills, which are practiced during class and dance showings. They need to be a respectful, aware, feeling, and responsive audience.

 **Obstacle**

Helping students become informed dance audiences

 **Solutions**

- Clipboard critiques (see chapter 8, Clipboard Critiques, pages 165 through 167) have been most beneficial. for keeping the students focused on the performance. Their writings reveal their opinions about the performance. The students comment on their observation of dance elements, meaning or feeling of dance work, what worked, and what didn't work. Not only does this method teach them to be a good audience, but it also affects their dance performance.
- By fifth grade the students have had many experiences as dance audiences and performers. Their final project is a solo performance of their choice that is 60 to 90 seconds long. The work illuminates their knowledge and appreciation of dance. As performers, their dances express meaning, depth, and creativity. As audiences, they have learned to observe dance with open minds, they are captured by the ingenuity of their classmates, and they are able to critique the meaning, technique, and performance while considering the the dancers' feelings.
- Over the years, my students established rules for being an audience:
  1. Observe the performance.
  2. Be open.
      See the entire work.
      Find meaning in the work.
      Ask why.
      Understand differences in genre and style.

3. Be respectful.

> Don't engage in personal conversation.
>
> Treat the dancers as you would want to be treated when you perform.
>
> Don't leave the room unless it is a dire emergency.

4. Respond

> by applauding,
>
> by laughing at the appropriate times,
>
> with awareness of cultural expression of the dance,
>
> by feeling!

These audience rules were not intended to squelch the students' responses to performances, but to alert them of appropriate skills and behavior for an audience.

Tip

Encourage your students to share the audience rules with their parents, who often do not know how to be a dance audience.

Trench Truth

In many schools audience skills are not used when the school has assemblies for speakers, orchestras, and plays. I taught in a school where the atmosphere was very relaxed. During assemblies most teachers and students were engaged in conversations about the speaker or performer. There was usually a low to very loud current of noise.

During a rehearsal for a formal program, I stopped several times to ask the students to be quiet. Then I realized that the classroom teachers were talking to each other and to the students. They felt like they were enjoying the process; I felt distracted by the noise. For several years I worked with each class to develop audience skills that focused on respect for the performers. The change was obvious and the level of focus for the audience and the performers improved but the teachers felt that it was a small school and that the personal level of communication was lost.

Afterword

And Now
We Dance

Reflecting on the past 11 years has brought home to me the struggles involved in developing a dance program. Class management and organization, parent–faculty communication, and working through the creative process were entwined threads. Although there were many mistakes made, a flexible and adapting program created an interesting tapestry of dance education. The program progressed to an exciting place from which to create dance. Here is a brief update on the program:

The views of dance expanded in the community. It was once considered a "girl thing," shaking the body, bump and grind, social dance, chorus lines, and Broadway dance. But parent–student dance classes and performances paved the way for parents to understand and respect the creative dance process. Now, most parents support creative dance and appear to enjoy its benefits.

Religious views in the community continue to affect arts programs. But the objections are usually in regard to arts performances and holiday celebrations. Most performances, therefore, have themes that are intended to be acceptable to the audience, such as farming, the weather, or the 20th century. However, students continue to be unable to attend dance classes because of religious beliefs. Administrative relations with parents and churches as well as parent visitation to dance classes proved helpful in communicating the goals of the dance program.

Communication between the dance specialist and the faculty is a daily requirement that includes reporting on student progress and integrating the curricula, or just talking about personal lives. Participating in the activities of the faculty, such as workshops, faculty meetings, and lunches, helps to build an understanding of each person and a respect for the teaching situation.

Most faculty members and administrators are supportive of dance. The effects of the dance program are evident and highly valued by the many classroom teachers. Connections between dance and the classroom curriculum are rewarding in that they raise awareness of the arts for classroom teachers. They see the effects the arts programs carry over to the classroom, especially in areas of respect and teamwork.

Much information in this book addresses class management. Yet, the most effective method for establishing class management was and is scoring of behavior (see chapter 3, Consequences, pages 49 through 53). Since scoring was introduced, the students' behavior improved beyond expectation. As a result, the reins are loosened because the students are focused on dance. The arguing and fighting among groups and partners virtually ceased as respect became internalized. The students are learning to be flexible while collaborating with team members.

With class management initiated, creating dance became the focus. The creative process is successful and is supported by the critique stage. Through critique, students quickly learned to focus on the dance task and to take ownership of their work. They were able to meet the standards for creating dances and looked forward to new challenges. As audience members, the students' ability to observe and appreciate dance and aesthetics of other cultures improved immensely.

The children experienced and witnessed so many different styles and forms of dance that dance is no longer a shock to their minds, bodies, and emotions. The giggling and embarrassment that they originally expressed are rarely seen anymore, and the students appear to be comfortable with movement. The students' fear and apprehension about the creative process has for the most part vanished and most students are eager to attend dance class.

The approach for creating dances remains distinct between boys and girls. The boys begin with ideas and movements, and the girls begin with organization. However, the differences between the ways that boys and girls moved lessened. Now, the girls take risks with their movement. They roll, leap, support weight, slide, slither, run, and move through space. In addition to these movements, the boys demonstrate contrasts in movement such as gentle and strong. They desire to be gentle, to be balletlike, to use scarves, to turn, to be as light as they are strong.

Puberty continues to sneak up on the fifth graders and appears to cause an overnight change. Opening their arms while freely twirling and leaping through the space are suddenly difficult for them. It is crucial to discuss this matter frequently. Although the process seems awkward, the students are assured that it is a passing stage. Moreover, they are inspired to dance their way to the other side of this stage.

The dance program has evolved into something new and wonderful. By some form of osmosis, the incoming students appear to understand dance and its goals. The teaching of dance elements and concepts is easier than it was in the earlier years, and the students are able to apply basic dance elements by first and second grade.

The dance atmosphere that was created propels us from the earlier years. A mind-set and motivation for dance is established. Student behavior is focused on movement tasks and creativity. The dance standards are being achieved. Without painting a fantasy world of dance in the public schools, I may simply say that the dance program has become effective and solid. And now we dance!

we dance rhythm
we dance on the beat and with musical phrasing
we feel it.

the dance built of form and structure has meaning
thinking is enhanced
connections
with literature, creative writing,
science, and math are clear
we strive to succeed
And we know.

we pool our thoughts
    apply the elements and concepts
self-confidence and pride fill our lives
the joy of creating is desired
    ownership, our own uninhibited movement
            we feel and know.

we leap,
    lift,
        toss,
we move together and in contrast
    feel the energy of the audience
        connect the energy of the dancers
we bow
    and we receive our applause
                and feel.

we are changed
we have moved to a new place in our lives
we will never be the same
                    For We Have Danced.

Appendix A

Performance Rules

Many aspects of performing are learned through years of experience. Performance not only requires appropriate etiquette, but it also assumes psychological and emotional readiness. Most students are not aware of performance requirements, and they will need much training.

Following are the rules that I teach over an extended time to prepare students for performance. Not only are these rules training for performance, but they also give students options for appropriate problem-solving techniques. These rules include explanations and actual narratives that I use while working with the students; and of course, I always demonstrate each of these rules with comic relief.

Be Ready

- **The dance begins when the audience sees you.** The audience usually sits in a semicircle around the performance space (thrust stage). The gym space has no wings to keep performers out of the audience's sight. As the students walk to their beginning dance positions they are in full view of the audience. Knowing that the dance begins when the audience sees them, the students are focused and silent.

- **The beginning and ending of the dance are crucial.** Because of the proximity of the audience, the dancers wait in stillness for their movement cue. At the end of the dance, the dancers either exit or freeze. When appropriate, a bow is rehearsed as the ending.

The beginning of the dance sets the mood. If you're talking to your friend or waving to your mom, the audience will not know whether the dance has started and whether they should be paying attention. At the end of the dance you'll freeze. During the freeze, count slowly: 1 banana, 2 bananas . . . 5 bananas. This long pause signals to the audience that the dance is completed. Then you'll bow and the audience will know to give you your reward: applause.

- **It is important to focus on your cue.** This means connecting what is happening in the dance with cues to move. For example, "Think to yourself, Five people slide across the stage . . . now the girls roll . . . Billy turns and leaps and then I go."

Have you ever watched a cat trying to catch its prey? My cat likes to catch moles. She will sit looking into the mole's hole for several hours. She will let nothing disturb her; she is totally focused on the hole. Eventually, the mole pokes its head out of the ground. The cat pounces and *zap!* She catches the mole. A cat's focus is what you need for performance. You may wait a very long time for your turn to dance, but you must stay focused. When your turn comes you are ready to pounce.

- **It is important to stay focused.**

During the performance it may become difficult to stay focused. Sometimes people in the audience yell out your name. If this happens, it can distract you from what you are doing. People may also be taking pictures or videos. That makes it more difficult to stay focused on your dance performance, but you must try!

This is a story that I share with fourth and fifth graders the day of the performance. The story is quite timely and acts as the fine-tuning before the performance.

Once when I was in school my history teacher, who was not feeling well, asked us to listen to a reading. I thought to myself, I'd better pay attention to what she's reading because she will probably ask us questions. The poor woman looks awful; I certainly don't want to upset her. I finished my thought to hear her say, "John Adams." The reading was completed that quickly. I had missed the entire thing because I was getting ready to focus on the reading. She asked a few questions and realized that no one in the class had paid attention to the reading. The teacher was very angry with all of us. The point of this story is that I was spending my time getting ready to focus. Focus means to be there; it does not mean to get ready to be there. In dance your mind and body must be connected with the moment.

Know How to Cope With Surprises

- **What if you fall down during the performance?**

Falling down happens all the time in performance. It even happens to the best dancers in the world. The problem with falling down is not getting up. If you lie there the other dancers will trip over you, the audience will get upset, and you will create a dangerous situation. If you fall down, don't sit there crying about it. Get up and keep dancing. If you do it fast enough, no one will even notice. If you hurt yourself, make yourself part of the dance until you can move off the stage. Then your teacher will take care of you. If you fall down and break a leg, lie still until the dance is finished. We'll call 911 (the emergency unit) to come for you.

This is a little dramatic, but for kindergarten through fifth-grade students the point is clear. My experience is that injury is rare at this level of performance. But I have seen children fall down, get up, continue dancing, exit, and then burst into tears. Usually, they wanted some comforting and acknowledgment that they continued in spite of falling. They were not physically hurt, but they wanted me to know that they accepted the emotional challenge to continue.

- **What if you're injured?** Depending on the age level and motivation needed for performance, I may talk about some Olympians who were injured and still continued to perform.

In 1976 the Japanese men's gymnastics team won the gold medal because of the valor of Shun Fujimoto. Shun was obviously in pain when he mounted the still rings, but he was the hope for his team winning the gold. During the dismount, which is a 9-foot drop, his face displayed excruciating pain. It wasn't until he appeared the next day wearing a full leg cast that the world knew he had performed on a broken kneecap! There's also the story of American Kerri Strug, who had severely sprained her ankle on her first attempt on the vault during team finals at the 1996 Olympics. The coaches thought they needed Kerri's score to win the gold. She was told to go for the second vault, which she did. She landed the vault perfectly and then fell on the mat crying in pain. The team won the gold. The point of these stories is for you to consider how much the performance is worth to you and your team.

- **What if you forget the dance or make a mistake?**

  No one likes to make mistakes, especially in performance. I have made mistakes, and you will probably make them too. Don't get upset if you make a mistake or if you forget your dance. It happens to everyone. The trick is not letting the audience know that you made a mistake. If you are doing a solo and you forget, you're lucky because you can create something on the spot. Create something until you remember what to do. If you are dancing in a group, simply look at the person next to you and follow that person until you can remember. No one will notice that you have forgotten—unless your mouth flies open, you slap your hands over your face, and your eyes bulge. Just keep dancing and no one will notice!

- **What if the music stops?** I always urge the students to just keep dancing and I will cue them no matter what happens. Recently, I had the surprise of my life. During a second-grade performance for the parents, half of the students sang "Chicken Soup with Rice" and the other half danced. Suddenly, the sound system died. The music teacher looked at me, and my eyes shot back at her. I scrambled to check the wiring and the sound system. The children just continued to sing and dance as if it were planned. It was amazing.

- **What if your shoe comes off?** In class we learn to continue the dance until it is finished. Before we start the warm-up or a show- ing of work, the students are instructed to check their shoelaces. If shoes come off or come untied during the dance, I remind them to move carefully and wait until the dance is finished before tying them or picking up the things that fell. With group movement that is free form (not choreographed movement), the students are allowed to move out of the dance space to tie shoes.

  If your shoe comes off while you are dancing, keep dancing. If your hat comes off, keep dancing. No matter what happens, stay focused and keep dancing. At the end of the dance you can pick up all your clothing as you exit. The audience is not coming to see you dress on stage (unless it is a dance about getting dressed). The audi- ence is coming to see dance.

- **What if you're in an embarrassing situation?** The following story acknowledges that there may be times when students feel embar- rassed, and it also helps children learn how to solve problems on the spot. Sharon's story is one that I share with students when they ask the what-if questions, such as "What if my pants fall off?" and "What if my shirt falls off?"

This happened when I was about 10 years old. It was in the days before Velcro®. We were in a dance recital for an audience of 2,000. Sharon, who was about eight years old, was performing a tumbling solo. She was dressed in a two-piece costume that resembled a bathing suit. About midway through her dance, the snaps on the top part of her costume broke apart while she was flipping through the air. When she realized what had happened, she began to chassé and skip around the stage, pressing her arms down to keep the top from falling. She signaled to the pianist to play her off, which he did. Poor Sharon—she was so embarrassed, not because the audience had seen anything but because she was in such a difficult situation. I hope you are never in an embarrassing situation. But if you are, you need to know how to keep your dignity.

Know Where to Go

- **Be aware of the boundaries.** The students become aware that boundaries exist in every dance space. I usually emphasize that crossing these boundaries is like falling into the orchestra pit of a theater. During class the caution cones or painted lines on the floor define the boundaries. The space is expanded or reduced periodically, so the students learn to make adjustments.

- **What if you're on the wrong side of the stage?** Should you run to the other side? Curtains serve many purposes on stage. Using a crossover is one way of getting to the other side during a performance when there is no sky drop or cyclorama. A child may realize that he is on the wrong side of the dance space when there is no sky drop or cyclorama. If the child panics, he may run to the other side unaware of the audience and the performing dancers. This is dangerous for everyone involved. In discussions about performance space, the students become aware that the dance space or stage is not a hallway. Discuss other possibilities of when and how to cross to the other side of the stage.

- **What if someone's in your space?** Should you push that person out of the way? Arriving in the wrong space is a common mistake that children make in the excitement of performance. They need to solve problems during the performance without pushing others. Quickly adapting to inconsistencies during a performance is a problem-solving skill. Through discussion, students become aware of the alternatives and will be able to make on-the-spot adjustments.

Know How to Deal With Nerves

- **What if I get butterflies?** The following is a story that I dramatize for students in kindergarten through second grade. I discuss the concept with the older students.

    Some children say that they have a tummy ache before they perform. Well, it feels like a tummy ache, but it's just butterflies inside. They're not real butterflies, but happy feelings, and I call them butterflies. These butterflies are so excited that they try to get out. If you sit there crying, "Oh, my tummy hurts," the butterflies will only hurt more and more because they want to fly away. To let the butterflies out all you have to do is begin your performance and give a big smile. The happy feelings—the happy butterflies—will come flying out and you'll feel good all over. These happy feelings are very important because without them you may not have the energy to do a good job. So when you feel those butterflies in your tummy, be happy because that's how you're supposed to feel. I will feel butterflies and all the other children will feel them too.

- **What if I need to use the rest room?** The students should realize that many people who perform feel the need to use the rest room.

Discussion about the need reduces the parade of students who want to walk out of the performance because they are nervous.

Many times when you know that you will perform next, you feel as if you need to go to the rest room. It is a common feeling. Usually, the thought of going to the rest room leaves your mind when you start to dance. One way to solve this problem is to go to the rest room 10 minutes before the program starts. Since the performance is only about 40 minutes long, you probably will be able to wait until the end of the show.

If you do not discuss rest room needs before a performance, there may be an incident such as the following. In a program organized by a group of classroom teachers, the rest room issue was not addressed. Five children were featured playing the piano. The music teacher relinquished her piano bench to each of the students as they took turns playing the piano. One girl whispered to the teacher that she had to use the rest room, and the teacher signaled to her to be quiet. Again, the girl whispered her need, and the teacher told her to wait. The girl was last to play, and she waited quietly. She played flawlessly and returned to her place with the other students. The music teacher returned to her bench. When she sat down she discovered that the cushion was soaking wet. The music teacher began to play and, because of the seepage, she didn't leave her bench until the entire audience had gone home.

Control Yourself

- **Scratching, picking, wiggling.** The objective here is to make children aware of unnecessary movement, not to make them neurotic. During rehearsal I may call attention to the scratching or wiggling. The students are usually surprised at how much they wiggle. Their spirit is simultaneously light and insightful.

   The audience is there to see you dance and hear you sing. The audience doesn't come to a program to watch you scratch, pick your nose, twirl your hair, suck your thumb, or cry. Some of you wiggle and scratch so much you look as if you have fleas. Although waving and blowing kisses are cute, you can wave anytime. The performance is the time to quiet yourself and focus. For the young children a wave or a kiss are usually choreographed in the dance.

- **Stillness.** In the thrust-stage setting, the students wait in a still shape for their entrance. If the dancers are waiting in the wings (which don't exist in this setting), they stand with their attention forward and their arms by their sides. I usually suggest that they hold the seams of their pants so their hands will be in control.

- **Quiet.** I tell students that it should be quiet backstage with this story.

   While you are waiting for your turn, don't talk. Respect the person who is performing. If you are talking, it could distract the audience or the person on stage. When you perform you want the audience to focus on you, not on the person who will follow you. Use the time to mentally prepare to dance. That means think about what you will do in your dance. When you have finished your performance, don't leave the stage screaming, "I did it," or laughing about the mistakes you made. Instead you need to go quietly back to your place. That is the hardest part: not talking when you have completed your work. You can talk after the program.

- **Stage lighting.** The students rehearse in the lighting that will be used for the performance. They need to experience the heat and the brightness of the light.

   The lights will shine brightly on the stage so that everyone can see you. Don't look into the lights. Try not to squint or block the light out of your eyes. Look away from the light. You won't be able to see the audience because they will be in the dark. But you'll know that they are there because they'll applaud.

Note: With the small stage lighting system, it is possible to see the audience. (See chapter 9, Rehearsing, pages 179 through 181.)

Know That Your Performance Is a Gift

- **Commit to the movement and offer the gift.** Although there are different purposes for dance, my objective is for the dancers to fully give of their talents and skills.

  The dance is your gift to the audience. Expend energy. Send your energy into the space so that all who feel it will be touched by the experience. If you are going to perform, commit yourself to the movement. If you feel shy or foolish, step on the other side of those feelings and dance full out. If you portray those foolish feelings, you will look foolish; but if you step beyond the foolish feelings and commit yourself to the movement, you will convince the audience and take them into the magical world of dance.

  Please don't offer the gift and then drop it on the floor. Think of your performance as presenting a banana split. Don't just show the treat and

then hide it. Let the audience taste the whipped cream, the nuts, the cherries, and the toppings. Allow them to dig as deeply as they want, getting down to the ice cream and bananas. Let the audience enjoy the gift. Commit to the movement.

- **Receive the gift.**

    In the giving of gifts, there is usually a thank-you involved. In the performing arts, applause is the thank-you. It is a wonderful feeling that is usually reserved for performance. You rarely get applause for doing well on a math test or for reading a story—unless you are performing it.

    Sometimes, the audience laughs while you are performing. This usually means that the audience is enjoying what you are doing. They probably think you are cute or funny. Enjoy that moment with them.

- **Accept and give compliments.** When someone tells you that you did a good job, thank that person. Do not say, "Did you see all the mistakes I made?" If a compliment makes you feel good, think of how another dancer will feel if she receives one from you. You can compliment each other.
- **Promote a sense of accomplishment.** A goal of performance is for the students to realize that the hard work they put into the creating, reworking, and rehearsing of the dance was worth it. They have arrived. They have brought their ideas to fruition!

Appendix B

Lagniappe

Lagniappe is a French term that means something given gratuitously. The following humorous and dramatized stories are a little gift that I'd like to share with you—*lagniappe*. The stories endorse class etiquette. They address some basic factors of class management, expectations, and groundwork. Many of the stories are in reference to bodily functions because everyone has experienced these and they are usually very funny to young children. The stories instruct students on when to drink, where to vomit, earthquake drills, and pencil throwing.

Water Story

The water fountain in the gym was a big distraction when I started the creative dance program in the school. I certainly didn't want to deprive children of water if they needed to drink; nevertheless, there had to be a limit to the traffic at the water fountains. In the beginning of the school year, I tell the following story.

> Ladies and gentlemen, you will notice that across the room there are two water fountains. At the end of class we will take time to drink enough water to float a ship. However, during the class I would prefer if you could refrain from drinking from the fountain. Usually, when one person drinks someone else gets thirsty; and there's a chain reaction. Before I know what is happening the whole class is racing to the fountain, gasping and shriveling up from dehydration. If you have hiccups or a bad cough, please come and tell me that you need a drink. If not, please wait until the end of the class.

About 100 years ago when I was a little girl your age, I lived in New Orleans where it was very, very, very hot. My dance teacher would not let anyone drink during class. Although it may sound insane now and not scientifically healthy, she taught us a very important lesson. All performers tend to get nervous to some degree. When this happens the salivary glands do not always produce enough spit. Dancers need to learn to breathe and relax in order for the salivary glands to work while performing. She told us to learn to "make spit." She wanted us to know how to do this because when you are performing you can't say to the audience, "Excuse me; I'll be right back. I need to get a drink." You will need to know how to make spit. This is a story from the old school of teaching; but it has been an important lesson to me as a dancer. So I want to share this opportunity with you. If I let you drink all the time, you will never learn this important skill. If you are desperate to drink for some reason, please let me know; otherwise, we'll wait until the end of class.

Vomit Story

The story that follows actually occurred my first year of teaching in a classroom. It was an incredible year during which I learned how to bend the rules. I act out this story for my students in order to impress upon them the need to vomit in the bathroom and not in the dance space. Second and third graders seem to love this story and beg for me to retell it year after year.

I need to let you know that whenever I see, hear, or smell anyone vomit, I start gagging, and I almost vomit myself. Did I ever tell you the story of Edie Vomdebter?

Many years ago I taught first grade. There was a little girl named Edie in my class. She had red pigtails and freckles, and she reminded me of Pippi Longstocking. Edie was very thin because she didn't like to eat. Edie's mother was very worried about her. Her mother insisted that she eat a hot lunch and asked me to check her plate to be sure that she had eaten everything. I knew that this was impossible. I changed the rule for Edie and told her that she only needed to taste everything on her plate.

One cold day in November, all the other children finished their lunches and were waiting to return to the classroom. Edie hadn't tasted anything. Because we were very late and trying to hurry along, I told Edie to take the plate with her. When we got back to the classroom, Edie put her plate on her desk. She sat there staring at it for 5 minutes. Suddenly, there was a big commotion: "BBBLLAAAAHHHHH!" Edie vomited all over her plate. The boy sitting on Edie's left saw her vomit and he vomited all over his desk. The boy on Edie's right also saw the episode. He jumped up to tell me that he felt sick, but instead he vomited on his desk, down the aisle, across the front of the classroom and down the hall. My glands began to salivate, and then I gagged and had tears rolling down my cheeks. I yelled to the rest of the class, "Everyone get your coats—we're having recess." The school nurse, principal, and janitor rushed into the room to take care of the sick children and clean up the mess.

The point of this story is to let you know that vomit is contagious. So please, if you feel sick, don't come to me and say, "Dr. Dance, I feel like . . . BBLLLAAAAHHH!" If you do that, I will also vomit all over the room. The best thing to do is to run to the bathroom, which is just outside of the gym. If I see you run out, I will be right behind you to be sure you're all right and to get the nurse to take care of you.

Earthquake Story

The view from where I taught in the Northwest is a majestic volcanic mountain range. Although Mount Saint Helens last erupted some 20 years ago, the mountain is still an active volcano with steam streaming from its mouth. In addition to this natural wonder, the earth plates are prime for earthquakes. During the school year, the children have several earthquake drills. I try to prepare them for such crises with stories and discussion. I have found it valuable to give elementary school children information without terrifying them. I usually tell stories that children consider humorous. An example of such a story follows.

Does anyone know the name of the big mountain that we can see from the schoolyard? Well, last weekend, I drove up the mountain to see the volcano. The forest ranger told us about the volcano and how it blew its top 20 years ago—long before you were born.

When I got there I could see smoke coming out of the hole. The volcano has fire inside of it, and the heat from the fire mixed with the rain and snow that are falling causes steam and smoke to come out. Sometimes, it seems as if the mountain gets an upset stomach with all the fire inside of it. It starts to rumble and burp. When this happens, the land near the mountain shakes. The shaking is called an earthquake.

We hardly ever have earthqua1kes here. But if we did, the earth would shshaaakkke for a few seconds, and then it would be over. Today, we're going to practice what we should do if we ever have an earthquake while we're in the gym.

If the gym starts to shake, walk to the wall (the inside wall). Make yourself into a ball shape next to the wall, close your eyes, and cover your head with your hands. Keep your eyes closed because if the lights fall down or if the windows break, glass will be flying around the room and you don't want to get it into your eyes.

We probably won't have an earthquake. But if we do, you will be scared and so will I. The important thing will be for you to hear the directions so that you will be safe. Please, please, please, don't SSSC-CRREEEEAMMMM! If you scream, everyone else in the gym will start to scream. If everyone screams, you will not hear the directions. When you panic and scream, no sound can get into your ears. You cannot hear anything. When there is danger it is sometimes best if we can be very quiet.

When the earthquake is over, someone will come to help us get out of the gym. And we will all be safe.

Pencil Throwing Story

The following story is true; it happened to my classmate when I was in seventh grade. I usually tell this story to fourth and fifth graders when someone throws a pencil or other dangerous object across the room.

Many, many years ago when I was in seventh grade, the students were always getting into trouble by throwing things in the classroom. They threw erasers, paper airplanes, candy, paper clips, wads of paper, and other objects. Many of these students were caught and spent recess and after school in detention.

One day the teacher asked us to be on our best behavior so that she could get a book from the library. I guess she thought that it would be all right because the library was just across the hall. As soon as she stepped out of the room, John, who was in the front of the room, threw a pencil at Billy in the back of the room. Unfortunately, the pencil did not get to Billy. Instead, Mac looked up just as the pencil was thrown, and it went right into his eye. Everyone started screaming. The teacher ran back to the room and called for help. They had to rush Mac to the hospital. Mac became blind in that eye and had to have it replaced with a glass one. John was suspended. But the worst part was that John felt absolutely terrible and cried for days because he was responsible for Mac's blindness. After that incident, no one threw anything in the room again.

About the Author

Cheryl M. Willis, EdD, is an award-winning dance specialist. She has worked as a classroom teacher in the United States and in Libya, North Africa, and is currently a creative dance specialist in the public schools in Vancouver, Washington. She has worked as a reading specialist in K-12 schools, successfully owned and directed her own dance studio, and taught in a performing arts center for theater students. She also has taught dance at the college level and choreographed and taught at a performing arts center.

Dr. Willis is a member of the American Association of Health, Physical Education, Recreation and Dance and was named national dance educator of the year in 2000. She also belongs to the National Dance Educator's Organization.

Dr. Willis earned her doctoral degree in dance at Temple University.

*You'll find
other outstanding
dance resources at*

www.HumanKinetics.com

In the U.S. call

1-800-747-4457

Australia............................. 08 8277 1555
Canada 1-800-465-7301
Europe.....................+44 (0) 113 255 5665
New Zealand.................. 0064 9 448 1207

HUMAN KINETICS
The Information Leader in Physical Activity
P.O. Box 5076 • Champaign, IL 61825-5076 USA